English for Academic Research

Series editor
Adrian Wallwork
Pisa
Italy

This series aims to help non-native, English-speaking researchers communicate in English. The books in this series are designed like manuals or user guides to help readers find relevant information quickly, and assimilate it rapidly and effectively. The author has divided each book into short subsections of short paragraphs with many bullet points.

More information about this series at http://www.springer.com/series/13913

Adrian Wallwork

English for Interacting on Campus

 Springer

Adrian Wallwork
English for Academics
Pisa
Italy

English for Academic Research
ISBN 978-3-319-28732-4   ISBN 978-3-319-28734-8   (eBook)
DOI 10.1007/978-3-319-28734-8

Library of Congress Control Number: 2016934339

Springer Cham Heidelberg New York Dordrecht London

Printed on acid-free paper

Springer International Publishing AG Switzerland is part of Springer Science+Business Media (www.
springer.com)

Preface

Who is this book for?

This book is part of the *English for Research* series of guides for non-native English academics of all disciplines who work in an international field.

It is intended for non-native English speaking students who are spending some time studying outside their home country.

EAP trainers can use this book in conjunction with: *English for Academic Research: A Guide for Teachers.*

What does this book cover? How is it organized?

The chapters are not intended to be read sequentially and are not arranged in a specific order. This book is like a manual, to be dipped in to when needed. However, by reading the entire book you will be extremely well prepared for living and studying in a foreign country.

Chapter 1 answers the questions: What's like it to live in a foreign country? How will I feel?

Chapters 2-3 deal with face-to-face relations with other students and with professors.

Chapter 4 covers emails to professors.

Chapters 5 and 6 should help you to participate more effectively in lectures, meetings, workshops, study groups, seminars etc.

Chapter 7 outlines ways to have effective conversations and discussions both on and off campus, for instance at social events in conferences.

Chapter 8 offers guidelines to making telephone calls.

Chapters 9, 10, 11 and 12 cover understanding native speakers, pronunciation, listening skills, and translation. Versions of Chapters 8–12 appeared in the first edition (but not in subsequent editions) of *English for Academic Correspondence*.

Chapters 13, 14 and 15 are reference chapters on smileys and text messaging, useful phrases, and grammar (and vocabulary).

How are the chapters organized?

Each chapter has the following three-part format:

1) FACTOIDS / WHAT THE EXPERTS SAY
In most cases, this section is a brief introduction to the topic of the chapter. These sections can also be used by EAP teachers as warm-ups for their lessons. All the statistics and quotations are genuine, though in some cases I have been unable to verify the original source.

2) WHAT'S THE BUZZ?
This is designed to get you thinking about the topic, through a variety of useful but entertaining exercises. These exercises can be done either by the reader alone, or in class with an EAP (English for Academic Purposes) teacher / trainer. The final part of each *What's the buzz?* section is a brief outline of the contents of the chapter. The keys to some of the exercises are contained at the end of this section.

3) The rest of each chapter is divided up into short subsections discussing specific issues.

How should I read this book?

This book is designed to be like a manual or a user guide—you don't need to read it starting from page one. Like a manual it has lots of short subsections and is divided into short paragraphs with many bullet points. This is to help you find what you want quickly and also to assimilate the information as rapidly and as effectively as possible.

You can use the Table of Contents as a checklist of things to remember.

I am a trainer in EAP and EFL. Should I read this book?

If you are a teacher of English for Academic Purposes or English as a Foreign Language you will learn about all the typical problems that non-native students have when studying outside their home country. You will be able to give your students advice on how to communicate effectively with each other and with their professors, tutors etc. In addition, you will find opportunities for generating a lot of stimulating and fun discussions by using the factoids and quotations, along with the *What's the buzz?* exercises.

The teacher's book contains notes on how to exploit all the books: *English for Academic Research: A Guide for Teachers.*

How is the term 'Anglo' used in this book?

I use *Anglo* to distinguish native English speakers into two groups. *Anglos* refers only to those speakers who are native to the following countries: USA, UK, Republic of Ireland, Canada, Australia, New Zealand and South Africa. It does not refer to speakers in countries such as India, Pakistan, Malaysia and the Philippines, where often instruction in schools is given in English, and huge numbers of the populations speak English on a daily basis, but whose cultures are not Anglo.

The distinction is necessary because if I simply wrote native-English speaking professors, that could be interpreted as covering not just, for example, North American professors but also those in several Asian countries. This would be very misleading as the teaching styles and relations with students may be very different between these two groups. Having said that, not all Anglos of course behave in the same way, but what I say is probably best termed as a stereotype that is more often true than not.

What I say about Anglo cultures is not exclusive to Anglo cultures, but is typical of, for example, Scandinavian countries.

I am not suggesting that Anglo culture or speakers are in any way better than any other culture, but I simply use Anglo as a useful device to avoid me having to continually list the seven countries mentioned above. I apologize to anyone who might find this distinction superficial, inappropriate or in some way racist.

What other books should I read?

This book is a part of series of books to help non-native English-speaking researchers to communicate in English. Other titles that you might like to read (or at least download chapters from) are:

English for Academic Correspondence - this will tell you more about how to communicate with professors and other researchers.

English for Presentations at International Conferences

English for Writing Research Papers

English for Academic Research: Grammar, Usage and Style

English for Academic Research: Grammar / Vocabulary / Writing Exercises

If, when you have completed your PhD, you are planning to get a job either in research or in industry, then you will find the following book very useful: *CVs, Resumes and LinkedIn*. The book is part of the Springer series "A Guide to Professional English".

Other good books on the topic of being a student abroad are:

Academic Interactions - Communicating on Campus, Feak, Reinhart, Rohlck, Michigan Series in English for Academic & Professional Purposes

How to Survive your Doctorate, Matthiesen and Binder, McGraw Hill Open University Press

International Students' Survival Guide (HarperCollins)

Student blogs

To learn more about what life is like when studying abroad, student blogs are a great resource and fun to read (and will also help you improve your English). Here is one example: https://manchesterontheroad.wordpress.com/tag/erasmus/

The author

Since 1984 Adrian Wallwork has been editing and revising scientific papers, as well as teaching English as a foreign language. In 2000 he began specializing in training PhD students from all over the world in how to write and present their research in English. He is the author of over 30 textbooks for Springer Science + Business Media, Cambridge University Press, Oxford University Press, the BBC, and many other publishers.

Pisa, Italy   Adrian Wallwork

Contents

Chapter 1

Living in Another Country and Dealing with Cultural Differences

Factoids: Top 20 difficulties of attending university

#1 Avoiding misunderstandings and embarrassments on Facebook, WhatsApp etc.

#2 Balancing studying, coursework, friendships and family life.

#3 Being far from your support network.

#4 Coping with cultural misunderstandings.

#5 Dealing with different teaching styles.

#6 Dealing with selfish roommates.

#7 Feeling like an outsider.

#8 Finding somewhere to park on campus.

#9 Finding the energy to complete the course, particularly when you are near the end.

#10 Funding yourself.

#11 Getting the required reading done.

#12 Getting up early in the morning for lectures.

#13 Getting used to currency differences.

#14 Learning how to become independent and responsible for yourself.

#15 Making friends.

#16 Missing friends and family.

#17 Motivating yourself to study when you could be going to a party.

#18 Opening the fridge and finding there is nothing to eat.

#19 Overcoming the language barrier.

#20 Procrastinating.

© Springer International Publishing Switzerland 2016
A. Wallwork, *English for Interacting on Campus*,
English for Academic Research, DOI 10.1007/978-3-319-28734-8_1

1.1 What's the buzz?

1) The factoids on the previous page were taken from blogs and tweets written by A) native English speakers attending university in their own country, and B) by non-natives attending university in another country.

   - Which ones do you think belong to Category A and which to Category B, and which to both A and B?

   - Which ones have you personally experienced or do you think you might experience in the future?

2) Discuss these questions.

   1. How much previous experience have you had of living away from your home country / town?
   2. What difficulties do you think you might experience?
   3. How homesick will you be? How often do you intend to phone home to your family and friends?
   4. Apart from family and friends, what else do you think you will miss from home?
   5. How easily will it be to make friends? Are your new friends more likely to be from your host country or other foreigners like yourself?
   6. How easily do you think you adapt to new situations? How independent are you?
   7. How different do you think the organization of life on your new campus will be compared to your university/campus back home?
   8. Would you prefer to live with a) native-speaking students, b) people who speak the same language as you, c) other foreigners?

****

Living in another country is a wonderful opportunity to open your eyes and broaden your mind. Not only will you learn new ways of doing things, but you may well learn to see yourself and your home country in a different way.

Before you embarked on this new adventure, you may well have studied the websites of the university and of the town where you plan to go. Such websites tend to be written in a reasonably objective way and should give you some clear insights into your new home.

But when you arrive on campus in your new country and new university, it is advisable to reserve any pre-conceived ideas, and just concentrate on what you see with your own eyes and what you actually experience first hand.

The chapter is based on various interviews I have conducted with people who are not living in their home country. My aim is simply to give you an idea of

- what it is like to live in another country

- some of the cultural problems many students encounter

- how host students might interact with foreign students

- how important it is to try and let go of your own stereotypical views

Please note that I am only offering a few (often very personal and subjective) perspectives, other people might have had very different experiences.

KEY TO EX I

The ones that were taken from blogs and tweets from non-native English speaking students attending university outside their own country were: 3, 4, 5, 7, 13, 15 and 19

1.2   What is the difference between travelling around a country and actually living there?

There is a tendency to think that living in a place is just the logical extension of visiting a place and being a tourist. But everyday life in a foreign country entails dealing with the mundane: living permits, work permits, opening bank accounts, getting a mobile phone number, finding a flat etc. What you often suddenly realise, particularly if you don't speak the language, is how difficult it can be with out the support of friends and family.

When travelling you make friends along the way, spend a night or a few days together, and then carry on your way. And the friends you make tend to be travellers like you - full of curiosity with fun stories to tell and advice on where to go next. But when you are living in a foreign country, you cannot rely on others who speak your language who happen to be passing through your town. Establishing relationships with the locals will help you develop a sense of belonging. But making such relationships is not that easy.

The cultural experience of living in a foreign country is also very different. When traveling, what impacts on you most is often the cultural heritage of a country and also its food. When you live in the country, you tend to be more affected by the social norms.

When you are communicating in a foreign language, your ability to judge people and their intentions becomes impaired. When you are dealing with a conational, you have a series of parameters for instantly making a judgement about someone - for example, you can get a good idea of their background just from the way they speak (their accent, their tone, the words they use). Within 30 seconds you probably have a fairly accurate, although superficial idea about a person. You have to start all over again to gain the same intuitive capacity in a foreign land.

But all this potential frustration is actually just the beginning of a fascinating voyage of discovery. Not only of the country and its culture. But of yourself.

1.3   I am not sure about whether I would like living in another country. Is there any way to simulate the experience?

Understandably many students are not sure whether they are ready to commit themselves to three years' (or more, or less) studying in a university in another country. You may be worried about not having your family and friends around, about eating very different food, living in a different climate, experiencing a very different teaching style etc.

One way to 'test out' both the country and the university is to apply to do a summer school there. Summer schools promote exchanges between students, researchers and professors from different institutes, regions and countries. By attending a school you will:

- see the different teaching styles and standards of professors in that country compared to your own

- meet many students who come from that country, and thus probably get an idea of actually how similar they are to you

- learn about the local culture, taste the food, visit a few places

By gaining insights into the pros and cons of living in another place, and discovering that the pros will almost inevitably heavily outweigh the cons, you should be well equipped to decide whether studying abroad would be a good thing for you.

And of course in addition to the interesting cultural experience, a summer school is a fun place to learn more about your particular field of research.

1.4 What typical difficulties do people encounter when living for a period abroad? How long does it take to get used to living in a new country?

A lot of students underestimate the initial difficulties of living in a new country. When you live in a foreign country, you do not spend your time in cafes or looking at the artistic or natural heritage. You have to make friends. And to do that you have to speak the language. If you don't, you find yourself dependent on others to do even the most mundane tasks - post a letter, make a bank transfer, get a work permit, pay a bill. It can be very frustrating and quite demeaning at times, especially when you have to express yourself in the most simple terms as you haven't yet mastered the language. It may be of some consolation however to know that everyone goes through this process and that your experience will improve, especially if you make the effort to get to know local people.

Remembering the feeling of nerves when you arrived and feeling completely out of your depth should fade away within a few weeks, but there are still challenges amongst many positive aspects.

Initially, you are often hit hard with all the differences (both positive and negative) from living in another country. Small things can often be the hardest! Asking for things in shops or restaurants can prove to be really challenging and overwhelming when you are so far away from the familiar. Another major challenge is making new friends and building relationships when you are not always sure of what is culturally appropriate.

Habits may be very different, for example, people's concepts of personal space and privacy vary massively from country to country.

However, when such cultural aspects become more familiar and relationships are formed, it becomes much easier to enjoy life and really see the richness of the local culture. Initially you have to get used to a new job, a new culture, new friendships, new languages and it is normal to want to pack your bags and go straight home! However if you can endure this, it will hopefully be a wonderful experience and one where you as a person will grow a lot and learn a lot about yourself and how you adapt to new and sometimes uncomfortable situations. There is definitely a feeling of pride that comes when you realize that you have stuck at something, even when initially it was very hard.

6

1.5 What do I do when the initial excitement of living in a foreign country wears off?

It can be hard when the initial excitement of being somewhere new fades and the reality of daily life takes over. It's important to keep up contact with people back home and if possible, schedule in trips to visit your home country in order to feel re-energized and ready to get stuck in to your new way of life again.

However, while it is initially worth staying in touch with people from home (i.e. to remind yourself that you do have good friends), it is also beneficial not to over do this. Too much time on the phone or computer might mean that you miss a lot of good opportunities to meet new people!

Sometimes having to push yourself into new situations can be a great way to grow from a personal perspective, enabling you to meet people you might normally never have met.

1.6 Will the teaching style of professors be different from that in my home country? Are student-professor relationships different?

This very much depends on where you come from.

In any case, some typical characteristics of universities in Anglo (see Introduction for a definition of 'Anglo') countries are:

- professors expect their students to interact during class and challenge their ideas. In your country you may be used to always accepting what your professor tells you and not to ask questions - see 3.4 and 5.2

- professors expect their students to (learn how to) think critically and independently

- a whole topic is covered during a lecture, and this constitutes examinable material. In other countries much of the materials needed for an examination will only be provided in textbooks and thus accessible for independent learning

- exams are written (oral exams only for testing foreign language competency)

- more focus on practice than theory

- relationships with teaching staff tend to be more informal (but not less professional) - see 3.3

- emails with professors are common, but should be reserved for vital questions that require the professor's expertise- - see Chapter 4

For more on this important topic see Chapters 3 and 5.

1.7 What things will I have to do on arrival at my university?

There will be orientation events, which are welcome events when university departments provide information to the new students.

Can you tell me where I should go for the Freshman/Orientation events?

Where are the Freshman / Orientation events taking place?

You will have to register for the courses you wish to take.

Excuse me, can you tell me what documents I will need to register for the courses?

Which courses are compulsory? Which courses am I required to enroll on?

How many credits are there for the course on …?

Are there any online courses that I should consider?

You will probably need to go and see the student support services.

Where is the student support office?

How do I get a doctor?

What documents do I need to get a bank account?

Am I insured to do laboratory work?

Is there any accommodation that I could have on campus while I look for a flat in the town?

I am not sure how to complete this rental application form. Can you help me?

Where is the local mosque?

Is there free Internet?

How do I get a travel card?

Can you recommend where I can buy a second-hand bicycle and a lock?

You may wish to join student associations.

> I am interested in rock-climbing. Are there any clubs I can join?
>
> I would like to get involved with decisions regarding university policies. Is this possible?
>
> Are there any political groups on campus?
>
> Is it possible to learn a martial art?
>
> What are fraternities and sororities?

1.8 What student services are typically offered at universities?

Many universities offer support in the following areas, when you:

- are having difficulty keeping up with a particular course (there may be a tutoring service available or a peer-to-peer mentoring program)

- can't decide what extra courses you should be taking (an academic advisor should be able to help)

- need to write or revise a paper (in this case there may be courses available, but see the companion volume *English for Writing Research Papers*)

- have personal problems (there should be a counseling service available)

- have financial difficulties (go to the financial aid office)

- need ideas about what to do when you have finished your degree (go the career planning office)

In such cases you could say:

> I am having a problem with … [*mention the specific problem*].
>
> The thing is … [*introduce more details of the problem*]
>
> Do you have any services available that might be able to help me?

Other services that are available are not just for offering support. Instead, they may be organizing events: music, dance, theater, sports etc. It is a good idea to get to know all the services your university offers, and whether they are free of charge or not. You can find this information from fellow students or from your department's / university's website.

1.9 I have read a lot of contradictory information about the host country on the Internet – how do I know what to believe?

A typical way to find out about another culture is to read books, articles and blogs about it. However, in order to retain their readers' interest, the authors tend to focus almost exclusively on the differences, rather than on what two cultures have in common.

Below are some 'facts' about Italy taken from a book called *Buying a House in Italy*.

- Most restaurants have bright fluorescent ceiling lights and a TV blaring.

- Black prostitutes line the roadsides.

- Men urinate in public.

- Pornography is on display at child height.

- Religious, almost pagan, respect for the dead.

The book gets excellent customer reviews on Amazon (all 5 star, apart from two 4 stars), which would seem to imply that the book contains information that readers find interesting or useful. However, given that I myself live and work in Italy, I would say that that the above five facts are not representative at all of Italy. Instead a much fairer and more constructive list of 'facts' would be:

- Children are adored and restaurants are extremely child-friendly.

- There are markets everywhere with local produce.

- Educated adults can talk with authority about almost anything from history of art to philosophy to politics.

- Most people talk about their hometown with a great sense of pride and affection.

- Italian homes tend to be extremely clean.

In fact, the problem is that my five facts are not sensational, they don't make a book interesting. My facts also contain elements that could be true of many countries, i.e. things we have in common with each rather than the differences. In order to find the differences, however, journalists and writers often have to focus on rather narrow sectors of the society of a country. That is why, for example, non-British people often tend to concentrate on the British royal family and the aristocracy (who actually make up a tiny percentage of the country) rather than the average person who may offer little in terms of offbeat interest. To an English person like myself, this seems very strange - in my family we rarely, if ever, talk about the royal family, and certainly with not much affection, which is contrary to the expectations of our non-English friends.

When you arrive in your new country, it pays to look for the things you have in common. This attitude will also help you in your professional life. Tom Southern is an Englishman who is the CEO of an American company based in Sydney Australia, which is active in South Asia (so four cultures involved - American, English, Australia and South Asian). He says:

> We've traditionally dealt with a lot of Asia Pacific groups, and those groups have usually been represented by natives of their own country. Our attempts in those markets have been to try and focus on any aspects that would bring different cultures together. So it was very much looking for small similarities and not really spending a lot of time worrying about things that were clearly quite different. What's happened with the Americans in many respects is that people make the immediate assumption that the Americans and British, and Australians are essentially very similar types of culture, with the same type of business approach. And that is often a pitfall because what seems to happen is that rather than understanding the similarities between us, that gets discarded. Instead what we notice is the differences. And although these differences which might only be a relatively small percentage of the total picture, they become the thing that you focus on. So bizarre as it may seem, we actually find there is more conflict, or more potential for conflict, with these American businessmen than there probably is with any of our Asian partners.
>
> We also learn a lot from our Asian partners' ways. For example, the Japanese don't necessarily enter a discussion or meeting expecting to come up with a solution. On the other hand most of the western world is very task orientated. For the Japanese, the answer will arise from the individuals participating in the discussions and in allowing time to come up with the right solution.

Moral of the story: Look for things you have in common. Focus on the benefits of those things that you do not have in common.

1.10   Should I re-evaluate any stereotypes that I have of my host country?

We inevitably go to other countries with an idea in our minds of how the people there are and how they behave, and whether we are likely to enjoy being there or not. We are also very much affected by what other people tell us.

However, it is important to remember that no two person's experience will be the same. You only have to look at reviews of places on Trip Advisor to see how travellers can have totally different experiences in the same hotel, same town, same country.

Below is the experience of Andrew Flint, who moved from Manchester (UK) to Siberia in order to teach English.

I was prepared for being in the middle of nowhere, but I found a surprisingly normal place. It is the people who are different.

Siberians (they make a distinct differentiation between themselves and European Russians) are very misunderstood in my opinion. Before I arrived here, I was one of many who believed they were a closed, unfriendly people, but the complete opposite is true. I often compare English and Siberian attitudes to my students, and the best way I can describe it is that Siberians are very honest. By that I mean that if they don't know you and don't want to talk to you, they will ignore you - this is really not considered rude, because everyone understands and accepts how people interact - but if they do want to talk to you, you will be invited into their homes, provided with a sumptuous meal and generally made to feel like a long-lost friend. I have found the stereotypical English attitude of putting on a smiling face regardless of your opinion of other people a little misleading - when is someone being genuine?

The pros? Learning something new every day about how Russians think and treat each other; having an endless source of new things to discover; learning a completely different language; but most of all, living somewhere that very few people from England have ever been to. The cons? No cinema with English sound; extremely volatile weather (the hottest time of year reaches +35 degrees Celsius, in deep midwinter it can reach minus 40); it is difficult for friends or family to visit - the bureaucracy and visa system here makes any visit a huge ordeal; a 6-hour time difference makes communicating with my family via Skype, and watching live sport, problematic; premium alcohol, electronics and clothes are very expensive.

All in all, I couldn't have found a better place to live ... a fascinating country that continues to surprise me.

Andrew's story highlights how important it is to ignore stereotypes and build your own impressions.

1.11 What typical cross-cultural conversations am I likely to have?

Below is the transcript of a recording between a Scottish woman (Scot), a Canadian man (Can) and an Englishman (Eng) on the stereotypes that they find they have to 'suffer'. At the time of the recording the three speakers were in London, England. The conversation is typical of a conversation you might have on your own campus.

Scot   It really amazes me how Scottish people have attracted the reputation for being mean [*not generous with their money*] because I find that any Celtic communities, whether it's Irish or Scottish in comparison with the English are instinctively very generous. On a very practical level things like for example measures in pubs. If you go into a Scottish pub you're served a third of a gill [*a measurement for liquids*] or a quart of a gill. If you come to England, you're lucky if you get a sixth of a gill.

Eng   I wonder where that's come from actually, this fallacy about the Scots being mean. I wonder where that began.

Scot   I don't know whether it's to do with the fact that we're very nationalistic so we tend to sort of hone in together [*form a cohesive group*] and blame the English for everything that goes wrong in our lives.

Can   It's interesting. There's a friend of mine who's Glaswegian and works in finance and she says that it's definitely an asset for her to be Scots and working in finance because of other people's perception of her. They perceive her to be good with money.

Scot   Yeah, they perceive you to be wise with it and not extravagant. So yes in some ways that is good, although it's a misconception. The other thing is people, I think Scottish people can be very direct and honest, and I think that is a very positive quality. But other people take offence at that. They perhaps feel that English people don't always say exactly what they mean, they skirt round things [*don't go directly to the point*].

Can   In some ways it's very interesting being a Canadian citizen because Canada is one of those countries that has an image of being a boring kind of cold place, which isn't really accurate depending on where you live in Canada.

Eng   My image of Canada is that it's very very clean but I also think that everybody in Canada swans [*goes*] around in jeans and big cowboy hats, and rides horses all the time.

Can   Well that's not so far off [*quite close to the truth*] but I think people forget that a huge portion of Canada's population is actually urban and the smaller places in Canada are indeed very very small. Ninety five per cent of Canada's population is within 100 miles of the American border and lot of people really forget you have this enormous country with nobody in it. There are huge urban centers like Toronto and smaller ones like Vancouver on the coast. So most people lead an urban life.

Eng   I think English people also think that Canadians are very serious and intellectual people, that's often seen as a strong thing with Canadians.

Can   I think Canadians a national sense of kind of insecurity. It's partly because we live next to a very populous, very very powerful country that dominates our culture and dominates everything we do. This is one of the reasons why so many Canadians don't want to, for instance, get rid of the Queen as a national head of state, which in fact the Queen still is.

Scot And what about the French situation with Quebec?

Can   The Quebecar are very hot [*it's very important for them*] on being Quebecar because it makes them different from America and from the rest of Canada.

Eng   But that's similar to us over here in Great Britain with you know the Irish, the Welsh, the Scottish and the English. I think with English people what frustrates me is that we're perceived as having a stiff upper lip [*never complaining in the face of adversity and unemotional*] and not being able to show emotion. I don't think that that is true. As a nation I think we've developed to the point where we do show emotion.

Can   Well, all countries are in a state of evolution.

Eng   They are. But the one thing I do think's true is we're supposed to drink lots of tea … and I do!

The transcript highlights that:

- every nationality is a victim of stereotyping and that no one enjoys being stereotyped

- understanding your own nationality traits / characteristics may help you when interacting with people from other countries

- having a conversation about different cultures often reveals things you may have never thought about before and can therefore be very stimulating

1.12 How do I deal with the stereotypes that the other students might have of people from my country or if I am being victimized because of my nationality / race?

One of the most moving moments I have ever had in my teaching career took place in 2015, just before the 'historic' signing of the agreement between Obama's government and the government of Iran. An Iranian PhD student of mine asked me in the break of our lesson if she could stand up say a few words to her fellow students (made up of Indians, Ethiopians, Spanish, German, and Croatians, but with a high percentage of Italians - the course was taking place in Pisa, Italy). I should mention that Italy has historically always had a good relationship with Iran, and was one of the few European countries that maintained a consulate there during the 'axis of evil' period.

Basically, she and fellow Iranians at the university, had been the victim of stereotyping and in some cases racism (landlords refusing to rent out rooms to Iranian students). The essence of what she said was that any foreign visitors to her country were welcomed, they were considered as guests and were treated as such - Iranian 'hosts' would go out of their way to help a stranger. She had not found the same welcoming attitude in Italy or indeed anywhere in Europe. Secondly, she brought up the fact that nearly everyone made no distinction between Iran and Iraq, assuming that they were basically interchangeable words. She wasn't criticizing her fellow students on the course, in fact she was one of the most popular students in the class, but was simply trying to raise their awareness in the hope that what she said might be spread around the university and the town.

A couple of weeks later, her parents were in Italy to visit her and her brother (also a PhD student) and they invited my wife and I out for a meal. We sat down and wine was ordered. My wife and I looked at each other, and I said 'no, actually I have to drive so I won't be drinking' - I had imagined that they had ordered the wine in our honor and that they as Muslims, would not be partaking. Instead they insisted, and poured us and themselves some wine. They could see the look on our faces and said "Oh, we're not Muslims". My wife and I, both had the same thought 'they must be Christians' - in fact Christianity has a long history in Iran, with more than 300,000 worshippers at the time of writing. It transpired that they were all atheists. Despite believing that we are very open minded and socially aware, my wife and I were both shocked at ourselves for not having thought of this immediately.

The moral of this rambling anecdote is:

- never assume anything about another person - they may or may not fit your stereotyped vision

- don't equate the policies of a country's government as a reflection of the people living there

- be aware of the importance that people have of belonging to a particular country - no Canadian appreciates being called an American, no Scot likes to be called English

- if you are a victim of stereotyping, try to open the eyes of the people around you by unpacking the stereotype with them to see what lies within

If you are the victim of racism, however mild, inform the student representative of your course. Try to encourage all the students to meet and discuss their cultures. A good way to do this by cooking typical national dishes and eating together - sharing cooking methods and ingredients is a great starting point for discussing different cultures.

Avoid forming cliques of students of the same nationality, or groups of all the non-host country students and those exclusively of the host country. University courses are a perfect environment for being curious about the people we share the planet with.

If some elements of cross-cultural discussions become too personal or for whatever reason too difficult, then you can politely refuse to answer 'difficult' questions (see 1.13 to learn how).

1.13   How should I deal with questions that I do not want to answer?

The following questions are typical of the kinds of questions citizens of the US get asked.

1. Doesn't the fact that more than 50 % of women go to work have a negative impact on the family?
2. Why do you seem to have little respect for your elders?
3. What are you doing to combat your gun, violence and drug problems?
4. Americans don't score high on world geography - why??
5. How well-informed are average Americans regarding not just home news but also international politics and world events?
6. In US elections why is there so much focus on scandal and finding dirt about candidates?
7. In what sense is there an 'American dream' when some of the world's richest people live alongside some of the poorest?
8. What right does the US have to act as if you were the governors of the world?

You might like to think of the typical 'difficult' questions people could ask about your country, and then think of possible answers to them or indeed whether you would simply say:

I really don't have any opinion on that.

That's an interesting question, but I don't think I am qualified to answer it.

That may be, I couldn't really say.

I'm afraid I don't know anything about it.

It's not really for me to say.

It depends how you look at it.

I'm sorry, I don't want to go into that.

Or alternatively you can revert the question back to the questioner:

Why, what do you think about it?

Do you think it is always best to avoid asking controversial questions? If you are asked a controversial question what tricks do you use to avoid having an argument?

For more on asking and responding to 'controversial' questions, see 2.7, 2.8 and 7.15.

Chapter 2

Relationships with Fellow Students

Factoids

❖ Students at the University of York in England drink more alcohol than any other university in the UK - the equivalent of nearly five liters of lager per week.

❖ In the US, the average college student attends 62 parties per year.

❖ Brigham Young University in Provo (Utah, USA) holds the record for being the US university where you are most likely to meet your future spouse.

❖ Students in the USA of Asian origin tend to be considered to be more studious than other students, while 'American' students tend to ask more questions in class.

❖ Undergraduates in the USA often form fraternities and sororities, which are single-sex organizations for male and female students, respectively. The names of these groups are often taken from Greek letters (alpha, beta etc) and their members are sometimes known as 'Greeks'.

❖ The University of Cambridge in England has over 400 registered clubs and societies for students.

❖ The Indira Gandhi National Open University located in Delhi India has the highest number of enrolled students - nearly 3.5 million. The top 10 universities by student numbers are located in India, Turkey, Iran, Pakistan, Bangladesh, Indonesia and Nepal.

❖ Estonia holds the record for the highest proportion of female graduates - more than two thirds are women.

❖ It costs a minimum of $300-400 per month to cover living expenses while studying in Russia.

❖ The Japanese word *ronin* means a 'masterless samurai' and refers to those students who fail the entrance examination to their university of their choice, and then spend an entire year or longer, studying for a second attempt to gain entrance.

❖ Michael Kearney is the US's youngest ever college student. At the age of 10 he was awarded a bachelor's degree in anthropology from the University of South Alabama.

© Springer International Publishing Switzerland 2016
A. Wallwork, *English for Interacting on Campus*,
English for Academic Research, DOI 10.1007/978-3-319-28734-8_2

2.1 What's the buzz?

1) An icebreaker is a question or statement designed to 'break the ice', i.e. to start a conversation. Look at the icebreakers below, decide which ones you might use yourself when talking to a fellow student who you haven't met before and who is sitting near you in class for a course whose first lesson is today.

   1. Do you know what time we're supposed to finish today?
   2. It's so cold here don't you think?
   3. Did you see the match last night?
   4. Were you at the freshmen's party?
   5. Where's everybody else?
   6. Do you know anything about the prof who's taking this course?

2) Imagine you wanted to find out information from a fellow student about the following:

   • where to get a good pizza

   • an inexpensive vegetarian restaurant

   • cheap places to buy food

   • cafès

   • music venues

   • bookstores

   • sports halls

Think of a question you could ask about each place, excluding asking for details about their location and how to get there.

3) Imagine you are just about to start a new course with a professor (instructor) you know nothing about. Who and what would you ask to find out:

   • what the instructor is like

   • how much help the instructor gives participants

   • how difficult the course will be

- how much preparation is required

- what attendees need to bring with them to class

- what kind of assignments the instructor gives

- how interactive the class is

- who will be on the course

- when the exams are

- what grades students normally get

- what happens if you miss class

******

This chapter deals with how to establish a relationship with other students. It covers

- how to introduce yourself and break the ice

- typical areas of conversation and areas to avoid

- establishing a sense of solidarity with other students

- being curious about where people come from

- understanding what is and is not acceptable to talk about

More details on the mechanics of having a conversation can be found in Chapter 7.

This chapter does not cover: relationships that become more personal, the norms for how close to stand to someone when talking to them (personal space), the norms for touching/hugging and kissing/greeting other people. These aspects are outside the scope of this book, but are nevertheless key aspects of life on campus.

To learn more see Chapters 5 and 6 in the *International Students' Survival Guide* published by HarperCollins and available online.

2.2 How should I introduce myself?

You can introduce yourself in various ways.

Hi.

Hi. Richard.

Hi, I'm Richard.

Hi, I'm Richard Jones.

Hello I'm Richard Jones.

Good morning I am Richard Jones.

Anglos say their first name (*Richard*) followed, in more formal situations, by their family name (*Jones*).

If someone from the academic staff asks *What is your name*? you would normally reply with both first and family name, but with a fellow student you can just say your first / given name.

Anglos often give their own name rather than directly asking the interlocutor for his/her name. This may take place several minutes into the conversation, particularly if the conversation appears to be worth continuing. A typical introduction is:

By the way, I'm Kalinda.

By the way, my name is Kalinda Abbas.

Sorry, I have not introduced myself - I'm Kalinda Abbas from Pakistan.

At this point you would be expected to reply with your name.

Pleased to meet you. I'm Zahra Rahman. I'm from Iran.

If you didn't hear the name of the person you have just been introduced to you can say:

Sorry, I didn't catch your name.

Sorry, I didn't get your name clearly. Can you spell it for me?

Sorry, how do your pronounce your name?

Don't be reluctant to ask for a repetition of the name. We all like it when people remember and use our name, we feel important and consequently we are more responsive to people who remember it.

2.3 What questions do students typically ask each other when they have just met?

Three typical question areas are: i) where you are from, ii) where you are living on campus or in town, iii) which courses you have signed up for. It is important not just to ask the question, but also to comment on the answer or ask a follow-up question (to learn more about this see Chapter 7.5).

Here are three example conversations - they should read vertically not horizontally.

So where are you from?	So are you living on campus?	So what other courses have you signed up for?
From Estonia.	No, actually I am sharing a flat with some friends.	Statistical analysis, IPR, sustainability economics …
Estonia. Pardon my ignorance but where is that exactly?	Oh really, so you're living in the town?	Wow I am doing exactly the same ones. We'll be seeing a lot of each other!
Eastern Europe near Russia. And you?	Yes, what about you?	

Note how the initial question begins with *so*, which is used to signal that you want to introduce a new topic. Note also how in the first two examples, the person who was initially answering the questions, ends by saying *and you?* - the idea is to have a balanced conversation rather than a police interrogation!

Be careful not to ask questions such as:

What are your hobbies?

What plans do you have for the future?

Which football club do you support?

The problem is not the questions are impolite - they are not. But if you ask such questions you are making the implicit assumption that your interlocutor has specific hobbies and specific plans, or is interested in football. Such questions are not very appropriate as conversation starters and are better rephrased as:

What do you like doing in your spare time? Do you have any particular hobbies?

So, do you have any particular plans for the future?

Are you interested in football? Do you support any particular team?

However, if a topic such as football has already been introduced into the conversation then you could ask a more direct question:

So which football club do you support?

Again, the use of *so* at the beginning of a question helps to make the question less direct.

Such exchanges enable you and your interlocutor to:

- get used to each other's accents and style of speaking. You are not giving each other essential information, so it does not matter at this point if you do not understand everything you say to each other

- find your voice in English

- make a connection with each other

- learn a little personal information that you might be able to refer to in future conversations

- make some positive comments about each other

To learn more useful phrases when first meeting someone see Chapter 14.11.

2.4   How can I find out more about my fellow students?

One way of making friends and learning new things at the same time is to find out what students study who are outside your own research group.

You can develop a relationship by finding out more about what someone does and what they are interested in and passionate about. It helps if you can think of good questions to ask them that will help you to understand the person better and at the same time strengthen a relationship.

Let's imagine that you met a student at a party and you found him/her very friendly. You later discover that he/she is learning sign language (i.e. the system of communication using gestures and signs by deaf people).

Think of five questions that you could ask him / her.

Now look at the conversation below between someone who is studying sign language (what they say is in *italics*) and another person (in normal script). As you read note:

1. which of your questions were asked
2. how the questioner shows interest
3. how the questioner uses the other person's answers to take the conversation forwards

You will need to read the piece at least twice in order to analyse the three points above.

So you're learning to sign. How are you getting on?

It's hard because signing is not based on the spoken language, so they say things in a completely different order. I think that when you have been used to doing things the same way all your life and you have to start thinking in a completely different way it's a real challenge.

I think people usually perceive deafness as being very limiting.

Yes, well I went in there expecting sign language to be quite primitive and discovered that there is an entire literature, poetry, plays, a whole culture in fact.

Presumably sign language is very visual.

Yes, you've got a lot of signs that paint a picture. The sign for a biscuit is bashing my elbow onto my left hand.

So how's that got anything to do with a biscuit?

A hundred years or so ago when a lot of deaf people were in institutions they used to give them such hard biscuits that they used to have to break them with their elbows.

So these signs have their own history?

Right.

Wow. And is sign language international?

No it isn't. We are used to thinking of American and British English as being pretty much the same thing so you can imagine it came as some surprise to me to discover that American sign language is actually much closer to French sign language than it is to British sign language.

To French? That's weird. And is there an equivalent to slang?

Yes, both slang and swear words. For example, you've got your thumbs up which is good, but if you put your little finger up that is bad, you know, vulgar.

So you can shock people using sign language?

Definitely, and I never thought that deaf people would be able to shout or sing. To shout they make much larger signs and more pronounced facial expressions. And I've watched choirs singing in church, and the signs, the movements change, they really become like song.

So can they even do other types of music, you know like rap?

Yeah, with rap they have a much punchier use of their signs. It takes a while for a hearing audience to get used to not focusing on the sound, but the movements are so fluid and full of meaning that in the end it kind of exists in its own right.

To learn more about conducting effective conversations see Chapter 7.

2.5   How can I establish a feeling of solidarity with my fellow students? i) coursework and exams

One way that people create strong relationships with each other is to share some experience of hardship or suffering, or by meeting a difficult challenge. When trying to create a new work group, businesses, sports clubs and schools often arrange team-building activities. Such activities can involved potentially dangerous situations such as climbing and sailing, where all members have to work together to ensure the safety of everyone and the success of the task.

In the world of academia such bonding (i.e. creating close ties with other people) is often unconsciously conducted by sharing the various difficulties of academic life - impossible assignments, impossibly difficult tests and impossible professors:

1. We had to answer 15 questions in less than 20 minutes.

2. What about that last question? How were we expected to know the answer?

3. It's almost like she wants to torture us.

4. Professor Mengel can be really mean in class, don't you think?

You also need to be able to answer such questions or comments. This shows that you are empathizing with the other person. Here are some possible answers to 1-4 above.

1. You've got to be kidding. / You've joking.

2. Exactly. / I didn't even bother trying to answer it.

3. Yes, torture us. It's either that, or this is her way to get us to study.

4. Well at least he's not as mean as that calculus lecturer.

Note the different answering / commenting strategies used: 1) reacting to something that you didn't share but which you can imagine; 2) agreeing, then saying what you did; 3) agreeing, then offering an alternative explanation; 4) mildly disagreeing and adding your own perspective.

You can also share in other people's difficulties (as in 1) above where you are not directly involved yourself. So if someone says *I have got to hand in the assignment tomorrow and I've still got 30 pages to write*, you can offer various reactions:

5. How are you going to manage?

6. That does sound a lot of work.

7. Can you not ask the prof for an extension to the deadline?

8. I had a similar problem last month, I went to speak to the prof in person, I think that's better than sending an email - it makes you seem that you are taking the problem seriously. In the end, she gave me an extra week.

In 5) and 6) you are just showing empathy. In 7) you make a suggestion, and in 8) you not only provide a solution but you also prove that your solution has worked (at least for you). In any case, in all four cases you show that you are a sympathetic listener and thus increase your chances of cementing the relationship.

You can establish better relationships if you ensure that the focus is not always on you. So if you have explained a difficulty and your fellow student has made his / her comment, then you can try and make him / her the focus by saying:

What about you, how are you getting on with the assignment?

I remember that you had the same professor last semester, how did you manage him?

2.6 How can I establish a feeling of solidarity with my fellow students? ii) everyday life on campus

You can use the strategies outlined in the previous subsection to bond with fellow students in non-academic situations as well.

Possible difficulties that students have on campus are:

- financial (the cost of accommodation, courses, food, alcohol, etc)

- difficulties with room mates (too noisy, too intrusive, poor hygiene habits, etc)

- health issues (allergies, intolerances, headaches) etc.

You can react by showing sympathy:

Yeah, that must be really hard / tough / difficult.

I can imagine how hard that must be.

Really? I am sorry to hear that.

That's too bad / really unlucky.

So how do you manage / cope?

So what happens when …?

2.7 Are there some topics of conversation that are not acceptable for particular nationalities?

What is appropriate varies from nation to nation. A Japanese woman told me:

In Japan we are hesitant to talk about personal matters. For instance, many British people I have met like to talk about their families and show photographs, but the Japanese don't do that, at least not in depth. We would say "I have a husband. I have a son and I have two daughters". Japanese men like talking about hobbies, golf, for example. We talk about food. Women even like to talk about what blood type they are.

Sometimes you may think that your interlocutor is asking too many questions, which may be also too personal. Most Anglos would not consider questions such as *Where do you work? What did you study? What did you major in? What seminars are you planning to go to? Did you take your vacation yet?* to be too personal. Such questions are merely a friendly exploration in a search to find things that you may have in common. The purpose of the questions is merely trying to find some common ground on which to continue the conversation.

Some questions would not be considered appropriate by most Anglos. For example:

How old are you?

What is your religion?

Are you married?

Do you plan to get married?

Do you plan to have children?

How much do you weigh?

Have you put on weight?

How much did you pay for your car?

If you want to ask a question that you think might be potentially difficult or embarrassing for your interlocutor, then you can precede the question or statement by saying:

Is it OK to ask about … ?

Do you mind me mentioning … ?

Can I ask you what you think about … ?

It seems that some people in your country think that … What do you think might be the reason for that?

See also 7.15.

2.8 What comments do I need to avoid that might offend students/professors from my host country?

Universities in Anglo countries tend to promote equality, tolerance and free speech. This means you will hear people (even in lectures) freely expressing their opinions for example about:

- women's rights

- gay marriages

- atheism

- birth control and abortion

- racism

- sexual orientation and practices

- politics

You may or may not have strong views about the above topics, and these views may or may not be conditioned by the cultural and moral values of the country where you grew up. However controversial or offensive you might find these subjects to be, it is a good idea not to express yourself too strongly as this may have a negative impact on your relationships with other students and with your professors. You can simply say:

In my country most people have a very different perspective on this.

The above sentence is quite neutral as you are not revealing whether you agree with the perspective or not.

Most of your fellow students and professors will appreciate it if you do not make racist or sexist statements, and if you at least appear willing to hear another side to the story. It is generally a good idea to avoiding trying to 'convert' someone to your views.

And of course, you may find that your fellow students make racist comments about people from your country or are very critical of your government. In this case, again try to be diplomatic and polite.

2.9   What do I do if someone says something I don't agree with? How can I be diplomatic in my response?

If your aim is to build up a relationship in a harmonious environment then it is worth bearing the following factors in mind.

- If someone says something that you don't agree with, but the point they are making is not really important, then there is probably no benefit in contesting it

- If someone says something that is not true (but which they themselves clearly believe to be true), e.g. some erroneous data, they will probably not appreciate being confronted directly with the true facts - you will simply undermine their self-esteem

- Most people do not appreciate someone casting doubt on their opinions and beliefs, and are more likely to be even more convinced of their beliefs if these beliefs are attacked

If you decide to disagree, then try to find some aspect of what your interlocutor has said that you can agree with. State this agreement and then mention the area where you disagree. This shows that you are at least trying to understand their point of view, and that your intentions are not hostile.

Speaker A: Your government seems to be in a complete mess at the moment.

Speaker B: I know what you mean, and there are a lot of people in my country who think so too. Some progress is being made in any case. I don't know if you've heard that …

Note how Speaker B avoids using words like *but, nevertheless*, and *however* (*Some progress is being made* rather than *But some progress is being made*). Frequent use of words such as *but* may put your interlocutors on the defensive and they will simply come up with more evidence to support their initial statement. This could then lead to an embarrassing argument.

If someone says something that you believe is not true, then a good tactic is to be diplomatic and say something like:

Oh really? I may be wrong, but I'd always thought that …

I didn't know that. What I heard / read was that …

2.10 How can I avoid sounding rude?

In your own language you are generally aware of when you are being impolite. You know what little phrases you can use to sound polite. The problem of not knowing such courtesy forms in English is that you might appear abrupt or rude to your interlocutors. A native speaker may be surprised by your tone because in other contexts, for example, when you are describing technical details or in writing papers / letters, you may appear to them to have a strong command of English.

The secret is to try and show some agreement with what your interlocutor is saying before you introduce your own point of view. Let's imagine two people are discussing the relative advantages and disadvantages of nuclear power. Below are some phrases that they could use in order to express their opinions without being too forceful.

I agree with you when you say … but nevertheless I do think that …

You have an interesting point there, however …

I quite understand what you're saying, but have you thought about …

Water power definitely has an important role, but did you know that it actually pollutes more than nuclear power?

I agree with you, but I also believe that …

The sun is certainly a safe source of energy, but …

I know exactly what you mean, but another viewpoint / interpretation could be …

For more phrases on giving opinions see 14.8.

It is not easy to be diplomatic in a foreign language, so if you do inadvertently say something that produces a bad reaction, you can say:

I am sorry, it is very difficult for me to say these things in English.

Sorry, I tend to be too direct when I speak in English.

I'm so sorry I didn't mean to sound rude.

Sometimes you need to find a way out of a discussion or at least time to pause and think.

Sorry, I just need to make a phone call.

Sorry, I just need to go to the bathroom.

Can I just think about that a second?

Just a moment. I need to think.

Sorry, I'll have to check up on that.

For more phrases on this topic see 2.14.

2.11   How can I invite someone who I have just met to do something together?

If you feel that you would like to see a person again, at some point in the conversation you can say:

Do you fancy a coffee?

Shall we go get some lunch?

You must come over to my place some time, you can meet my flat mates.

Why don't you come round after the lecture this afternoon?

We're all going to a party tonight, do you want to come?

Possible replies to the above questions:

Thank you, I'd love to.

That sounds great, what time should I come?

Brilliant. See you later then.

Thanks but I'm already doing something tonight.

To learn how to refuse invitations see 2.12.

2.12 What excuses can I use for turning down invitations for social activities?

If you feel that you do not wish to participate in some social events, such as parties or dinners, then it helps if you can say something that will prevent your fellow students from convincing you to do something against your will. If you say something like *actually, I am really tired and would like to get to bed early*, the others can simply say *well none of us are planning to be late back* or *you can sleep during tomorrow's lessons*. It is much simpler to say something like *I am sorry but I need to stay in tonight*, without giving them any further explanation. If they insist, then just repeat the same phrase: *As I said, I need to stay in*.

However, if they do manage to persuade you, and you do decide to go, then you can say:

OK, then, I'll come.

OK you've convinced me—where are we meeting?

OK, but as long as we are not too late.

2.13 How can I avoid becoming socially isolated?

Before turning down an invitation (see 2.12) remember that being a PhD student can occasionally be a lonely experience in which you spend a lot of time working by yourself (either at your computer or in the lab). If you become socially isolated, this may end up making you less productive. If you don't like the idea of going to parties (maybe you don't dance or don't drink alcohol), there are plenty of clubs and associations you can join. Alternatively, you could get involved in community work.

2.14 What excuses can I use for ending a conversation?

If you find that your interlocutor is failing to interact with you and that the situation is becoming awkward, then you might decide to end the conversation by making an excuse:

Sorry, I have just seen someone I need to talk to. I'll catch you later.

Sorry, I've just received an sms—do you mind if I just take a look?

Do you know where the bathroom is?

I just need to get a bottle of water. Maybe I'll see you at the lecture?

Even if you have not had a long conversation, try to end on a positive note and thus leave a good impression with your interlocutor:

Well, it was nice talking to you.

Well, I hope to see you at the party tonight.

I'll try and make sure I come to your workshop.

I'll catch up with you later.

Chapter 3

Communicating Face-to-Face with Professors

What the experts say

The following come from *1001 Things Every College Student Needs to Know*.

1. Do not pick a professor because he's the funniest person on campus. Pick a prof whose students go on to get great jobs.
2. It's important to develop a relationship with your professor now, not a week before exams.
3. Professors don't have to get along with you. You have to learn to get along with them.
4. Sit as close to your professor as you can. It's easier for her to start recognizing you.
5. Just because a professor looks at you doesn't mean he's going to call on you. However, looking down at your toenails does tell him that you don't know anything.
6. You won't get as much praise from professors as you did at high school. College professors don't really care about your feelings or that you "worked hard" all weekend.
7. The "I didn't know it was due" excuse won't work now. Don't try it. You'll be laughed out of class.
8. It's not OK for professors to hit on you. Hitting on professors isn't advisable either.
9. It's as important to learn the instructor as it is to learn the material.
10. Take notes even when you record lectures. If you can't understand the professor in person, there's no way you'll know what he's saying on tape.

© Springer International Publishing Switzerland 2016
A. Wallwork, *English for Interacting on Campus*,
English for Academic Research, DOI 10.1007/978-3-319-28734-8_3

3.1 What's the buzz?

1) Read the factoids on the previous page and discuss which ones you: a) were already aware of, b) find useful, c) are not sure you understand.

2) Discuss the questions below.

   1. How do you typically address your professors in your host country? Is it the same way as you would in your home country?
   2. How do you think your professor would react if you used his/her first name? And how would you feel?
   3. In your country, how often are titles (professor, doctor, etc) used?
   4. In which cases would you go to see your professor (instructor etc) in their office (i.e. during their office hours): a) to discuss something they mentioned during a lecture that you didn't quite understand; b) to discover how to prepare for an exam set by them; c) to check some slides from a presentation or a section in a paper you are writing; d) to discuss a financial or family problem; e) to convince them to give you better grades; f) to discuss your career; g) to discuss changing course.
   5. Is simply going to see your professor to introduce yourself and to make sure that they know who you are a sufficient reason for meeting with them?

****

Every past and current student will tell you how important it is to interact with your professors, instructors, tutors, and advisors outside class. Having a good relationship with them will enable you to:

- discuss your progress

- get more from classes held by these people

- find more opportunities to carry out interesting research

- become part of their network and thus be able to access their contacts

If you are in the US, you can learn more about certain professors at your university by accessing: ratemyprofessor.com and pickaprof.com.

Note that in this chapter the terms *professor, instructor, tutor, advisor, lecturer,* and *principal investigator* will be used indifferently to mean anyone in an official didactic position with whom you have contact. In reality these terms have different meanings (which may also differ from university to university), but sometimes they may refer to the same person.

The term *office hours* refers to the official times that professors (instructors etc) are available to receive their students in their (the professors') offices.

Some of the early sections of this chapter exploit information contained in Chapter 4 *Interacting with Instructors/Advisors*, from the excellent book *Academic Interactions - Communicating on Campus* which is part of the Michigan Series in English for Academic and Professional Purposes. The book contains many examples of real dialogs between professors and students taken from the Michigan Corpus of Academic Spoken English, and is thus very useful to give you a feel for the 'real English' that is spoken on campus. The book also has an accompanying DVD.

Finally, note that a university is the perfect environment for improving your communication skills, and learning which form of communication is appropriate. When communicating with professors, you should avoid texting, WhatsApp and Facebook messages. Much of the time you will need to communicate with them face to face (this chapter) and sometimes via email (Chapter 4). Don't expect your profs to teach you how to communicate, it is up to you to learn, and this chapter should be a good starting point.

3.2 How should I address my professor / supervisor / advisor?

Every country has its own system of naming academic staff. If you are studying in the US you should be able to call nearly all those who teach and supervise you *professor*. In fact, most of them will be assistant professors, associate professors or full professors. So you can say either *Professor* or *Professor Smith* (i.e. his/her surname).

In the UK academics start their career as lecturers, then move to senior lecturer, and then finally to professor. When addressing lecturers and senior lecturers you can say *Dr Smith*, and for professors either *Professor* or *Professor Smith*.

In both the US and UK, if you are being taught by a post doc researcher, then you can say *Dr Smith*.

If you are worried about how to address someone, either find out from a fellow student or speak to someone in administration. Of course you could also ask the instructor / supervisor directly: *Sorry, but how should I address you?*

To learn how to address people in emails see 4.3.

3.3 My prof seems very friendly and informal. Can I be friendly and informal with him/her too?

Many non-native English speaking students who go to university in an English-speaking country such as the USA, UK, Canada, Ireland, Australia etc, may find that the professors there are considerably more informal than their professors at home.

This apparent informality may express itself in various ways. Your professor may

- invite you to use his/her first name

- make an effort to learn your name so that you don't feel like an anonymous student

- have a seemingly innate ability to listen carefully to your concerns

- show a feeling of genuine interest, warmth and caring

- invite you and fellow students out for lunch

- make jokes during class

- encourage students to interact with him/her during class

- freely admit to having made a mistake

- show students respect, and encourage them to express their disagreement

- try to maximize student success by for example before exams handing out review sheets with lists of topics they should know, and handing out practice exams.

- realise that he/she can have an important impact on your life and thus help you to develop your potential

However, what you consider to be informal or friendly, may in fact have nothing to do with informality. More likely it is the sign of a professional instructor who wishes to create a better relationship with students, and thus have more productive (and useful) students in his/her research group.

So, do not to confuse informality with a lack of professionalism. A professor can be highly professional and good at their job, as well as being informal.

Secondly, do not assume that just because a professor is friendly with you that that entitles you to be equally friendly with him / her. This is particularly true with regard to the emails that you send him/her (see 4.5).

3.4 How different are professors from Anglo countries compared to those from other countries?

I surveyed several PhD students who had spent time both in their home country and abroad. Here is a selection of their replies.

The first is from an Italian PhD student who studied for a period at the University of California and then at Grossbeeren, close to Berlin (Germany).

> My first experience abroad was in Davis, California. My professor was very friendly with me. Sometimes I was embarrassed about this because I had never experienced the same kind of familiarity with my Italian tutors. In my American lab, we used to spend at least one evening a week having dinner all together. It was normal to celebrate birthdays and public holidays, and each time my professor asked me to invite whoever I wanted. He introduced me to his wife and both his daughters and I spent Thanksgiving at their home. My lab in Italy was much smaller than the American lab and it was rare to spend free time with my supervisors, and we always had a very formal relationship.

> Regarding my stay in Germany, the professor who hosted me in her lab was very nice with me, but we did not spend a lot of time together since she was travelling very often. However, she had a very good collaborator who helped me every day. Every morning, all the people working there used to have breakfast all together. Unfortunately they used to speak in German all the time. They talked to me in English just to answer my questions. I think that the professor and her collaborator I met in Germany were the most qualified I have ever had, and both helped me a lot when I wrote my paper. The laboratories were also great!

The next student's home country is Iran, but she graduated from the Universiti Putra Malaysia. She commented to me that a professor's style or teaching and relationships with students doesn't always depend on the country, but simply on the personality of the professor.

> On my arrival in Malaysia I had an academic shock, not a cultural shock. My professor, a Chinese woman, dedicated a lot of time to explaining things to me. She gave me her email address and telephone number, and told me that if I needed to see her, I should book an appointment in advance. Whenever I hadn't seen her for a while, she called me, sent me text messages or emails. "Hi, Zahra. How is your research going?"

> Although I had worked at a university before, I had never liked the idea of being a lecturer or professor. However, she inspired me a lot and taught me how to understand things around me by being patient and respecting others.

Finally, another Italian student who also studied at Harvard Medical School.

I moved to Boston to spend six months as a visiting student in the Cardiovascular Surgery division of Boston Children's Hospital. I am in a really small lab (seven people), which is uncommon here at Harvard, where usually the labs have 30 people or even more. My current supervisor takes a lot of interest in his students: we have at least one lab meeting per week in which everyone updates the others on their own work. During the other days the principal investigator usually comes and asks how the work is going. If we have any issues he spends a few minutes brainstorming with each of us. This is really different compared to what happens in Italy! We don't have any regular lab meetings - it's random and rare for a professor to spend time with students! Another difference is the attention they pay to presentations at Harvard. My American supervisor focuses not only on the format of the presentation or the scientific impact, but also on the marketing aspect, as at some point we will have to sell the final product. My Italian supervisor focuses more on the scientific impact of the speech than on the business side. Regarding the level of formality, it is really high in both cases. Both of my supervisors - American and Italian - are really knowledgeable and smart people; they have the solution for any kind of problem, and you can learn a lot from them.

So what lessons can you learn from the above testimonies? I know it is a very small sample but in my experience it is indicative.

- Supervisors in the US may be more friendly, but no less professional, than professors from your country.

- Regular meetings between students and professors are more common in the US than elsewhere.

- Some supervisors can be inspirational, and this is completely independent of their nationality or location.

- If you go to a non-English speaking university, expect your colleagues to talk to each other in their own language.

3.5 What questions do I need to ask my supervisor when I first meet him/her?

Supervisors have different reasons for wanting to supervise the work and theses of PhD students. When you meet your supervisor for the first time, you should probably ask them some or all of the following questions:

First of all, how should I address you? (see 3.2)

I have a series of questions about how our relationship is going to work. Is it OK if I ask you them now?

Can I ask you what is your primary goal in supervising me?

You have read my research proposal, do you think my goals match your goals?

Realistically, how much will you be able to help me in carrying out my research?

For more similar questions see 14.4.

Basically the aim of these questions is to establish a transparent and balanced relationship between you and your supervisor. Later it will be your responsibility to keep your supervisor informed of your progress. Many supervisors dedicate a lot of time to their students, and it pays to show them plenty of appreciation. Others may be more remote and difficult to get hold of (i.e. difficult to contact and meet) - if you have such a supervisor you will need to work hard to establish a good working relationship as much of it will probably be via email or Skype. Always talk in positive and constructive terms, even if you become frustrated with the lack of face-to-face contact. It is generally a good idea to maintain a professional relationship and a certain level of distance - work will tend to be more productive in this way. So think carefully before moving into any kind of 'friendship'.

To learn more about how to deal with different types of supervisor, see Chapter 4 in *How to Survive your Doctorate*, Matthiesen and Binder, McGraw Hill Open University Press.

3.6   What do professors not like to see in a student?

You can improve your relationships with the teaching staff and instructors, by avoiding the following types of behavior. I asked a selection of professors in various countries what types of students they do not like. Here are some sample replies.

I do not like a student who ...

- is too friendly/doesn't show sufficient respect, and treats me as if I were a fellow student
- follows me around after class
- interrupts me while I am talking to someone else
- hands in assignments late and invents excuses for having done so
- cheats or plagiarizes
- plays with their cell phone during class
- never participates during lectures
- always sits at the back
- wants me to change the date of an exam or quiz
- looks bored
- is unreliable, frequently makes mistakes
- is not committed
- doesn't turn off their cell phone
- talks to other students during lectures
- does not take the research seriously
- is arrogant and always presumes to know more than me

- asks irrelevant questions during lectures and just wants to be the center of attention
- is unable to take constructive criticism
- wants help filling out routine forms
- always has an excuse for when they've made a mistake
- stares at me during lectures
- wants me to bend the rules
- doesn't put into practice what I've taught him/her
- arrives late
- starts packing up their books before the lecture is over
- expects me to teach them English
- asks me questions at the end of a lecture that could easily be answered by a fellow student
- emails me with unnecessary questions and requests
- communicates with me as if I were the same age as him/her
- stalks me on Facebook and forwards me jokes

3.7   What type of students do professors like?

Clearly, professors like students who don't commit any of the 'crimes' mentioned in the previous subsection. In addition, you could think about how you could help your professor and thus get noticed in a positive way. For example, all supervisors and professors appreciate students who help them with any manual/menial tasks such as entering data, compiling spreadsheets, doing tedious statistical analyses, preparing submissions for conferences, and doing library/literature searches. If you can occasionally help them with such tasks you will earn 'bonus' points with them. You can say:

I have got a couple of hours free this afternoon, if there is anything you need some help with?

More exciting or rewarding activities consist of helping them prepare manuscripts for publication or presentation slides for conferences. They may even encourage you to come up with new ideas and solutions.

Helping your supervisors and professors in such situations could also be advantageous when in the future you need a reference letter (see 4.12) from them.

My sample of professors wrote to me saying:

I like who a student who

- shows genuine interest in what I am teaching them or what I am talking about
- is enthusiastic and proactive
- is independent and can think critically
- generates ideas (whether they are practical or not)
- writes emails with a pertinent subject line, that are short, make sense, and are spelled correctly
- makes my life easier by arriving on time

- thanks me occasionally
- asks me for advice on how to achieve his/her (realistic) goals
- prepares for their meetings with me and never wastes my time
- only emails me when strictly necessary
- asks me for feedback near the beginning or middle of a project, rather than at the end (when it's probably too late)
- is prepared to help out with mundane tasks

44

3.8 How can I ask a favor face-to-face?

Asking a request face-to-face is less 'dangerous' than an email, as your facial expression, body language and the intonation of your voice clearly give the idea that you are being polite or at least are trying to be.

A typical way of making a verbal request to your professor is to catch their attention by saying:

> Professor, could I just have a word with you?
> Professor, could I ask you a favor?

Note that *could* is more formal than *can*.

Then you tell your professor the problem:

> The thing is I don't think I will be able to meet the deadline.
> I'm having some problems understanding …

Next you make your request:

> Could we possibly postpone our meeting till next Wednesday?
> Would it be OK if I was a couple of days late in handing in the assignment?
> Would you mind going through my presentation with me?
> Could you explain the final part of the analysis again?

And finally, where appropriate (e.g. in the request for help with the presentation and analysis in the third and fourth phrases above), you give the professor a 'get out clause', i.e. you make it clear that if for whatever reason the professor cannot fulfill your request, then you will understand.

> I realise that you may not have time. So if you can't, no problem.
> I realise that this is all very last minute, so I will understand if you can't …
> If you don't have time, then no problem.

An alternative tactic is to underline that the amount of work you are requesting from the professor is very minimal:

> It's really only a couple of slides that I need you to look at.
> I don't think it will take more than five minutes of your time.

3.9 How can I make the most effective use of time spent with my professor during office hours?

'Office hours' refers to the times when professors are in their offices and are officially available to see students.

Your professors, instructors etc will appreciate it if you find ways not to waste their time during office hours so that they can see as many students in as short a time as possible. Using their time efficiently will also improve your relationship with them.

The trick is to go to their office with your ideas well prepared: you know exactly what you want to talk about and you have studied the best way to explain this topic in English. If you think it could be a difficult or complex conversation with your professor, try to role play the conversation with a fellow student beforehand.

In addition, prepare any questions you think you might need to ask. The more specific the question, the more likely the prof will be able to help you effectively and quickly.

For example, instead of saying "I am having difficulty with xxx, what can I do?" you could say:

1. I am having difficulty in analysing the code flow with this code [*shows professor the lines of code*]. In the mpr.setFilter(function (row, a, b)) call, what are rows a and b? I can't find any variables by this name. Also how do the calls translate from one function to other? I know you explained a bit about this in class, but I am still not sure that I have understood.

2. In chapter six of my thesis I am comparing the psychological well being of identical twins as opposed to non-identical twins. Currently, I'm having problems with the data analysis. To be precise I am not sure what …

3. I am having some trouble with my fellow students. Basically, because I am not a native English speaking student, they tend to imitate me when I talk in class. As you can imagine, I find it distracting as well as quite offensive. I was hoping you might make a general announcement in class about it, as the problem not only affects me but some of the other non-native students too.

In examples 1 and 2, the student clearly identifies what the problem is and thus makes it easier for the prof to give an explanation. Example 3 refers to a problem of a personal nature. Note how the student appeals to the sensibility of the prof (*as you can imagine*) and also has a possible solution (*I was hoping you …*). In cases where you have already experienced a similar problem and the problem was solved, then you can suggest that the same solution could be adopted in the new case too.

3.10 How is an encounter during office hours typically structured? What particular phrases will I need?

First, try to ascertain if there is another student already with the professor. If not, knock and say one or more of the following:

> May I come in?
> Do you have a minute?
> Is this a good time?

Second, if you think the prof might not remember who you are:

> Good morning, I am Haana, the student from Iran. You may remember we met briefly last week.

Third, explain the reason why you have come:

> The reason I have come to see you is:
> I was wondering whether you could …
> Would you have five minutes to explain …?

Fourth, you have your discussion. It is a good idea to constantly check your understanding as you listen to the prof (see Chapter 9).

Fifth, when you have achieved your aim or your allocated time has finished:

> Well, thank you very much. You've been really helpful.
> Would it be OK if I came back at the same time next week?

Sixth, mention the next time you will inevitably be seeing the prof.

> Thanks again, and see you at this afternoon's workshop.

When you are leaving, you may remember that you had something else to ask as well:

> Sorry, I forgot to ask you about …
> Do you have another couple of minutes, because I also wanted to ask you about …

Make sure that you pick up on (i.e. understand) any signals that the professor might give you to indicate that your allocated time is over:

So, are we done?

So, does that answer your question?

Sorry, but I have to go now.

OK, so see you in class tomorrow.

In some cases, you might be the one who needs to get away:

Sorry to interrupt you Professor Smith, but I've got a class in ten minutes. Would it be OK to continue the discussion next week?

Yes, I think I've understood what you are saying. Unfortunately I need to go now because there's a workshop I need to attend.

3.11 What can I do to avoid 'bothering' my professor during office hours?

In the case of examples 1 and 2 in the previous subsection, before going to the professor, first check that you can't find the solution from another student. The idea is that you only 'bother' the prof when you really need to. Cases where you 'really' need to see your professor include:

- to introduce yourself to the professor for the first time (see 3.5) - it is essential that he/she knows who you are as soon as possible and as a result future communication will be a lot easier, and you are likely to get more eye contact from the prof during lessons

- to discuss an issue about your work that you cannot resolve simply by consulting with other students

- to clarify your relationship with the prof (if there has been tension between you) and your relative roles

- to discuss personal problems - but only if there is no one else in the department's staff who might be better equipped than your professor to talk about such issues

The result of only going to your professor in 'essential' cases is that he/she will take you more seriously and know that you have come to see him/her for a good reason. The same rule applies to writing emails to your prof - if the mail is not really necessary, then don't write it. Again, if you bombard your prof with emails, you are much less likely to get a reply.

Finally, don't expect your prof to solve issues that you could easily solve yourself. Instead of going to your prof to ask what additional courses you should be taking in order to accompany his/her course, and then expecting the prof to come up with suggestions, think of some possible courses yourself and check with him/her that they would be suitable.

3.12 Is it OK to go up to the instructor at the end of the class/lecture/seminar?

Most teachers are exhausted after they have held a couple of hours of lessons, so don't expect them to be particularly enthusiastic to find a line of students in front of them at the end of a lecture, seminar etc. Most will also have somewhere else to go - another seminar, a faculty meeting, the lab, lunch, home.

First, think if an email might solve the problem. This will depend on the type of question, and also whether the professor encourages students to send him/her emails.

Or could you simply ask another student or someone in administration?

If you really need to ask them something, prepare exactly what you want to say before, and express yourself clearly and concisely. Try to ask questions that will simply require a yes/no answer, or which can be dealt with in a few seconds.

You can say:

> Thanks for a great lesson. I was just wondering if you could tell me the name of the book you mentioned at the beginning of the lesson.

> I know you have to go now, but could I possibly meet you 10 minutes before the beginning of your lecture next Monday?

3.13   How do professors view people of different nationalities?

Be aware that your professors, like everyone else, tend to form impressions of people from other countries often based on limited experience and on what they have been told by other professors.

Here are some comments made by a Canadian English teacher on the differences between Chinese and Arab students. If you are Chinese or Arabic you may recognize some of these features as being true, but you may equally find them to be stereotypical or just plain wrong. Your job is to ensure that your professor has a true picture of who you are as an individual, rather than just an anonymous student from another country. That it is one of the reasons why you should try to interact with your professors as often as you can, so that they can really get to know you, and judge you for who you are rather than who they think you might be.

In general, I find Chinese students have a hard time with inferencing and critical thinking. They tend to be very good with concrete skills like comprehension of a reading or listening, or formatting or structuring a piece of writing or presentation according to a prescribed set of guidelines. If I ask these students to look a little deeper, perhaps at the subtext, or to be more creative in what they are producing, this creates a lot of anxiety in the student - they don't want to make a mistake/do something wrong, so they want to be told exactly what to do and how to do it.

In general, my Arab students tend to be more relaxed. I've been told by them that in academic studies in Arabic, they are required to infer the subtext in whatever they are reading/listening, so they are very comfortable also doing this in English. They also seem to be more successful at analyzing texts and evaluating the information to use in whatever they are producing. Where they tend to lack in skills is how to organize those ideas. The structure becomes cyclical with the general ideas never really narrowing to anything specific.

Obviously I've had exceptions with individual students.

3.14 What should I do if my supervisor asks me to do something I would prefer not to do?

As in every work situation, you may become embroiled in office politics. This may involve your supervisor asking you for favors or for things that may seem strange or even unethical. If you are ever asked to do something that you feel may not be appropriate or which you cannot understand the real reason for doing, simply say:

> I appreciate you asking me, but could you just give me a few days to think about it.
>
> Before giving you an answer, I would like to take some time to understand the full implications of what you are asking me.
>
> My initial reaction is to say yes/no, but please can you give me some time to consider it?

On other occasions, you may receive invitations of a more personal nature. If you wish to refuse an invitation you can say

> Thank you so much for asking me, but I would prefer not to.
>
> I am afraid that is something that I would feel uncomfortable with.
>
> My religion does not allow me to … But thank you anyway.

3.15 What can I do if a member of staff shows inappropriate interest in me?

The following letter appeared in *You - The New Woman*, an online women's magazine, published in English in Karachi, Pakistan.

> I am a 23-year-old university student and my problem is my professor who takes undue interest in me. I am just an average student but in his subject I get highest grades. In the lecture hall, he keeps questioning me particularly and ignores the brighter students who actually know the answers. I don't give him any encouragement; in fact, when I see him outside the classroom I don't even greet him. He just does not take the hint! I missed my classes due to fever and he asked my friends why I had not come. When they told him I was sick he asked them for my cell number. Now he pesters me with stupid forwarded texts all the time. I am sick of this situation and I cannot afford to misbehave with him either. He can fail me in the semester. On top of that I have to cope with snide comments by my class mates as well. Please give me some advice as I am worried about my reputation.

First, reassure yourself that the professor's behavior is in no way acceptable. Professors in your host country may be more friendly than professors in your home country, but they should know the boundaries between friendliness and inappropriate interest.

Your first tactic could be to see if other students are having or have had a similar problem. If they have, then you could go with other students to the student counseling office and explain the problem.

If you haven't already done so, try to ignore the professor and never be alone with him.

If you prefer to deal with the problem yourself, then find a moment at the end of a lecture, and preferably have another student alongside you, and say in a polite but firm manner:

> Professor, I would just like a word with you. I appreciate the fact that you have taken interest in me and that you seem to be giving me good grades. However, in my country such behavior is inappropriate. I find it extremely embarrassing and I would appreciate it very much if you could stop.

If the professor then leaves you alone and your grades remain the same, then you have solved the problem. On the other hand if he fails to leave you alone or he leaves you alone but there is a noticeable difference in your grades, then you should definitely talk either to someone at the student counseling office or to your tutor.

If you are getting undue attention from a fellow student, go with a male or female friend to the student and say:

> Hi, can I just have a word with you. I don't want to be rude or anything, but would you mind leaving me alone? The thing is in my country such behavior is inappropriate. I find it embarrassing and I would appreciate it if you could stop.

3.16   How should I behave with non-academic staff?

Universities in Anglo countries aim to treat everyone with the same respect: male or female; black or white; gay or straight; believer, agnostic or atheist; cleaner or professor; dean or secretary. You may become more friendly with certain people but this will depend on their personality (i.e. the reasons why you like them) rather than their role or position. Be polite with everyone.

Chapter 4

Communicating with Professors via Email

What the experts say!

The following humorous advice on how to write emails to (mathematics) professors appears on spikedmath.com. Clearly, it is not meant to be taken seriously!

1. Forget about using proper spelling or grammar. A lot of them learned English as a second or even third language, and the others forgot how to spell years ago.

2. Remember that mathematics is all about compactness. Get rid of extra words and try to use symbols whenever you can. Math professors LOVE symbols, like "u" versus "you".

3. Be sure to include MS Word attachments. Math professors like receiving attachments as it makes them feel special.

4. Send the email at a bizarre time like 4:53am. Math professors are almost always awake at this time doing research and will eagerly answer your questions as soon as possible.

5. Never write from your College/University email account. Math professors like to get to know who you really are, so just use your standard email account.

6. For subject, just put "NEED HELP ASAP!!!!" Professors have their spam filter set up to send your message into the spam folder if the subject line contains the course number.

7. Be as vague as possible so that your professor will provide as much information as possible. If you are too specific, they'll only answer one specific question. Why get one answer when you can get all of them!

8. Make sure you apologize if you missed a lecture. Don't forget to put an excuse. Basically any excuse will work since your prof has no way to check it.

© Springer International Publishing Switzerland 2016
A. Wallwork, *English for Interacting on Campus*,
English for Academic Research, DOI 10.1007/978-3-319-28734-8_4

4.1 What's the buzz?

1) Here are some short rules to writing and structuring emails. Read the rules and circle A, B or C according to whether it is a rule that you:

a) always follow; b) think you should follow, but don't; c) don't think is very important

RULE 1 BEFORE YOU START

Ask yourself:

Why am I writing this? A B C

Have I done everything I can to avoid bothering this person? A B C

What exactly do I want the outcome of this message to be? A B C

RULE 2 SUBJECT LINES

Use the subject line to say exactly what your email is about. It should be a maximum 10-word summary A B C

If you're reporting just a single fact or asking one question in your email, consider using just the subject line to relate your message. A B C

RULE 3 IDENTIFY YOURSELF

When contacting someone for the first time, always include your name and occupation (if relevant) or where you previously met this person. A B C

RULE 4 KEY INFORMATION FIRST

Your recipient will start with the first line to see if it's worth spending more of their time. Readers tend to pay less and less attention to what is written as they scan more quickly through the rest of the email. So to make sure the recipient reads the most relevant information, put this information as near to the beginning as possible. A B C

RULE 5 NUMBER MULTIPLE ACTION POINTS

If you are asking your reader to do more than one thing, number your points to ensure they are all read. Or consider sending important points as separate messages. A B C

RULE 6 WHEN ASKING FAVORS OR CRITICISING

In more delicate emails, always try to begin and end on a positive note. A B C

RULE 7 AVOID AMBIGUITY

Make sure you avoid ambiguity and that it is clear what pronouns (e.g. *this, that it, them, him, her*) and time references (*before, then, later*) refer to. A B C

2) Below are some examples of emails sent by students to their professors. Decide in each case i) whether an email was in reality the best form of communication, ii) whether the email is written in an appropriate manner and provides sufficient details. Note: the initial (*Dear Prof etc*) and final salutations (*Best regards*) have been removed.

1. Sorry for the inconvenience of sending this assignment (see attachment) late. Please can you give me some feedback.

2. Please could you let me know when the next lecture is. Thank you in advance.

3. As requested in your email, please find attached my assignment. I wasn't sure exactly what to write in the caption to the two figures - I would appreciate it if you could give me some advice on this. Thank you.

4. I have no idea what you mean by [*quotes prof's email*], maybe you could give us a clearer explanation. Hope you have a nice weekend.

5. I very much apologize but I am afraid that I will not be able to complete the assignment within the deadline that you mentioned at the beginning of the course.

6. Thank you for your course, it is both interesting and useful. I also appreciate the way you give us comments on our weekly assignments. Unfortunately I will be 48 hours late in sending you this week's assignment - is that a problem?

****

This chapter outlines some general rules for communicating with professors, instructors, tutors, advisors etc via email.

For details on how to write specific emails both to professors and outside institutions see the following chapters in the companion volume *English for Academic Correspondence*:

Chapters 1-3: subject lines, salutations, and structure
Chapter 4: choosing the right level of formality
Chapter 6: requests and replies
Chapter 7: summer schools, internships, placements, PhD and Postdoc programs
Chapter 8: reference letters

This chapter covers:

- how to address a prof in an email

- how to choose the most appropriate subject line

- whether to write friendly emails to your prof

- how to make requests, ask favors, and send reminders

- thanking and apologizing

- making phone calls with professors

4.2 What key points do I need to know about writing emails to my professors and supervisors?

Learning how to write clear effective emails is an essential part of your professional (and personal) life. University is a good place to learn how to do this.

Professors only have a limited number of hours in a day. This means they do not appreciate receiving emails that in reality do not require their expert input.

Below is some extremely useful advice given by Tom Stafford, Lecturer in Psychology and Cognitive Science at the University of Sheffield, England.

- If you email me a question which is readily available from a simple internet search then I am spending your tuition fees, and those of your fellow students, on being a slow and expensive substitute for Google.

- If you email me, please say your full name, level and, if relevant, which course(s) you are referring to. Although you know what "the lecture" or "the coursework" refers to, I may not. If you refer to an article, book or a webpage, please give the full reference and/or URL so that I know what you are talking about.

- I may not be bothered by you not including an introduction to your email, or by you not signing it, but many people you write to will be. You should also make an effort to capitalise, punctuate and spell correctly in your email. Again, although I may not judge you negatively if you fail to do this, many people will, so you should practise the habit of taking care over these things when you write.

- If you need a response by a particular time, it helps if you mention this in the email. If you have an urgent query (i.e. requires a response within 48 hours) email is not appropriate. Please call instead.

- I do not read my email over the weekend, or after 5pm.

- If we make an appointment to meet you must turn up on time. If you are late I may not be able to begin a meeting with you because it will infringe on other commitments. If you are unable to make an appointment, or are going to be late, please call to let me know, so that I am able to do other things with my time and am not waiting around like a lemon.

Other things to remember:

- Don't use abbreviations - spell out words completely. For example do not use *u* and *ur*, instead of *you* and *your.*

- Don't make demands.

- Immediately provide the context and then get straight to the request.

- The shorter the request, the more likely you will get a reply.

- Keep your sentences and paragraphs brief.

- Use white space between each paragraph.

- Don't think that your prof checks his/her email every five minutes.

- If you send an attachment, label the file with your name and give it some kind of title. Examples: *Genetics Presentation Yu Ling.ppt*; *CV Max Schmidt. pdf*

4.3 How should I address my professor, advisor, tutor (etc) in an email?

First you need to check what the official title is of the person you are emailing. In the USA most teaching staff are addressed as 'Professor', but this in not the case in the UK where professors only hold senior positions (those below them in the hierarchy are generally 'lecturers' - see 3.2).

So go on their webpage and see how they refer to themselves. If they give no indication then try and find out from your administration office.

As a general rule, if you are sure that the person is a professor then you can write:

Dear Professor Wallwork

(i.e. Dear + Professor with a capital initial letter + surname)

If you are not sure, it should be safe to write:

Dear Dr Wallwork

And this is how your email communication should continue. Even if the professor signs off with just their first name, this is not a sign to encourage you to write in the next email: *Hi Adrian, Hello prof ...*

Non-English speaking countries vary considerably in their use of titles from very informal (e.g. Sweden) to much more formal (e.g. Germany, Italy, Korea). In any case, you are unlikely to cause anyone offence if you use *Professor* or *Dr*.

To learn how to address academic staff face to face see Chapter 3.

Do NOT use the following titles: *Mr, Mrs, Miss, Ms.* There is a danger that you will choose the wrong one (either because you don't know the gender of the person, and/ or you don't know if they are married - which in any case should be irrelevant).

At the end of your email you can simply write *Best regards*. Phrases such as *Sincerely* and *Respectfully yours* are not used amongst Anglos. Phrases such as *Take care* and *Have a nice day!* would in most cases be too informal.

For more on salutations (i.e. the things you write at the beginning and end of an email) see Chapter 2 in the companion volume *English for Academic Correspondence*.

4.4   What subject line should I use?

Always write a subject line from the point of view of the recipient - in this case your professor, tutor etc. Professors spend most of their time doing three things: bureaucracy, teaching, research - bear this in mind when your write your subject line.

What is specific for you, maybe totally generic for them, and vice versa. Consequently, it would not be helpful in an email to a professor if you write a subject line such as *What time is tomorrow's lecture?* (However, the same subject line would be fine if written to a fellow student, who like you has only one lecture tomorrow). You shouldn't need to email your prof to find out the when a lecture is (consult your schedule, ask a fellow student), and given that your prof may have several lectures how can he/she know which one you are referring to?

So be as specific as possible. Some examples:

> Sorry, but can't make our 10:00 am appointment tomorrow (Tuesday).
>
> Attached is presentation on genetics for 0930 seminar on October 7.
>
> First chapter of my thesis for your review.
>
> Will get my first chapter of thesis to you by 0730 tomorrow (Friday).

Note that the above subject lines also act as a complete message, the professor doesn't even need to open the email. Note also that words and expressions like *tomorrow* or *in a few hours* can be ambiguous, as they depend on when the recipient looks at your message.

For more on subject lines see Chapter 1 in *English for Academic Correspondence*.

4.5 How friendly can I be with my prof in an email? How important is it to check the spelling?

My lessons with my PhD students are conducted in a friendly and fun way, which sometimes means my students think it is acceptable to write very informal emails to me, such as the following. This is not a good idea as the total lack of formality can be interpreted as showing a lack of respect.

> Hi Adrian
>
> how are u? amazing, I hope.
>
> Sorry to trouble u but I need a pice of advice from u: my professor Pinco Pallino (emeritus to UCLA University at LA) asked me to try to do some translations of his books for an editor from italian to english and I did: they said my translations was ok!! Can u image?? I was sooooo surprised!!
>
> Well, the fact is that I d like to have a final review of my translations from u.
>
> Could it be possible?
>
> How can I improve my level? Would u inform me about ur courses?
>
> Thank u in advance,
>
> Luisa

The unnecessary use of *u* and *ur* make it seem like you couldn't be bothered to write the full word. The tone is completely inappropriate and could be very irritating for your professor.

To a certain extent your emails are a reflection of you and how you carry out your research. My impression of the above student is that because she didn't take the time to check her email (*pice* instead of *piece*, *image* instead of *imagine*), she may not check her data when carrying out her research, i.e. the fact that she doesn't take the time to check her work (whatever aspect of her work) may mean she is not totally reliable.

The email below gives the impression that I already knew the student (I didn't) and assumes I will automatically help him out.

> Dear Adrian,
>
> I need help about my application for academic research project (proofreading about 600 words).
>
> I want to ask you
>
> > to estimate the proofreading duration and
> >
> > when you could begin to proceed my application.
>
> Any information you could give me would be very much appreciated.
>
> With best wishes,

The problem with the above email is not really the level of formality (although writing *Adrian* is inappropriate with someone with whom you have had no previous contact). The main issue is the total lack of information: who is the student? why would I want to help him?

4.6 Do I need to begin my email by asking how my professor is and other niceties?

No. Most professors would prefer to read your email as fast as possible, so there is no need to begin by saying: *How are you? Did you have a nice weekend?* The prof is unlikely to have the time to respond to these two questions.

Also, don't begin your email by saying: *Hey!*

Begin with a proper salutation (4.3) and forget any questions about health, weekend etc (unless you are on very friendly terms). However, such questions may be OK after a holiday, festivity, or when you haven't communicated with this person for several weeks or months.

4.7 How can I ask my prof a favor via email?

How you request a favor may determine whether the recipient will do what you ask. Here are some examples, which do you think are likely to be perceived as polite, and which sound like commands?

1. Please email me a copy of today's presentation.
2. Could you please email me a copy of today's presentation.
3. Could you please email me a copy of today's presentation?
4. Could you email me a copy of today's presentation, please?
5. Please could you email me a copy of today's presentation?
6. I was wondering whether you could email me a copy of today's presentation.
7. Could you possibly email me a copy of today's presentation? Thanks.

The first example is expressed in the imperative form. The imperative is often used for giving orders and is thus inappropriate when writing to your professor. The second example is a typical form of asking requesting, when the person making the requests is not really giving the recipient any choice - there is no question mark. This form is common between people of slightly different levels in a hierarchy (i.e. a project leader to someone in his/her project group).

Examples 3-5 are all expressed as questions, and thus sound more polite. The only difference is the position of *please*. The problem *with* please is that depending on its position in the phrase it can be interpreted as a command or a request, but not everyone agrees on what these positions are! Speaking personally, I prefer *please* at the beginning (example 5), as it reflects the position of *please* in many other typical email phrases e.g. *Please find attached a copy of ... Please feel free to contact me if ...*

Examples 6-7 are both polite and would never cause offence and so are both recommended when making requests.

For more on making requests via email, see Chapter 6 in the companion volume *English for Academic Correspondence*.

4.8 How polite do I need to be in my requests?

Very polite. Your supervisor or professor is not your servant. You <u>cannot</u> say for example the following:

> I need you to sign my attendance sheet. I will come to your office tomorrow.
>
> I want your help with my literature review. Attached are some questions. Please answer them.
>
> I need a reference letter. How quickly can you prepare one for me?

All the above are too direct and sound like an imposition.

Instead you need to show respect, empathy and appreciation. Below are polite versions of the three requests above.

> I know you have scheduled meetings tomorrow morning, but could I interrupt you just for 15 seconds for you to sign my attendance sheet.? Would it be OK if I came at around 10:00? Or after lunch at around 2:00?
>
> I am having some problems writing my literature review and I would really appreciate your input. I know you are very busy this week, but would you have 15 minutes to dedicate to me? Let me know when would suit you best. Thanks very much.
>
> As you know I am planning to apply for a summer school in Lima. Part of the admission procedure entails having two reference letters. Would it be possible for you to write a letter for me? The submission deadline is in three weeks (October 30), so if you could get it to me by the end of next week that would be great. Thank you so much.

The emails above highlight that you:

- should write in a reasonably formal style

- can show empathy by acknowledging that the prof is likely to be busy

- can give him/her an indication of how much time / effort would be involved in fulfilling your request

- should give your prof alternative times for meetings

- can conclude by thanking the prof

4.9 I need to request an appointment to see my professor / supervisor. What's the best tactic?

First explain the issue.

> I'm preparing the slides for the conference presentation.
>
> I am in the middle of writing the Discussion section for the paper and I am having some problems highlighting the level of innovation of our research with respect to the findings of other research groups.

Explain that you would like to meet.

> It would be great if we could meet to go over the slides.
>
> I was wondering if we could meet to look through what I have written so far.

Give the professor various options, not just one specific time.

> I am free any morning this week. So any time to suit you would be great.
>
> I am free this afternoon, all of tomorrow, and Friday morning. If you could find 20 minutes for me that would be perfect.
>
> I was thinking we could meet after class tomorrow afternoon, or if you prefer on Thursday afternoon.
>
> Would next Monday work for you to have a meeting?

All the phrases above would be suitable either in an email or face-to-face.

4.10 My professor hasn't responded to my request, what can I do?

When someone doesn't do something we ask them to do, a natural human tendency is

- to take it personally (i.e. we think the person is deliberately not responding to us)

- to think that the other person is incompetent

The result is that we often write impolite emails and thereby risk ruining our relationship with the recipient. The best strategy is just to assume that the recipient hasn't had time to do what we asked or that he / she has simply forgotten. In any case it is perfectly legitimate to send a reminder. The important thing is to be polite and not make any accusations or say anything that the recipient might misinterpret or find offensive.

You can write:

> *(1)* I was just wondering if you had received my email - *(2)* see below. *(3)* I know you must be very busy, *(4)* but do you think you could find five minutes for me *(5)* some time next week? *(6)* Thanks very much and have a good day.

The strategy is:

1. begin with a polite phrase
2. refer to your previous request by simply saying 'see below' - so after your signature you paste your original email. This means you don't need to say 'I have already sent you two emails', 'I originally sent you this email four weeks ago' - these two phrases are likely to irritate the recipient rather than encourage him/her to meet your request.
3. empathize with the recipient, i.e. show that you understand that they don't have much time available
4. minimize the amount of time that they need to dedicate to you
5. be flexible in when you could meet
6. end in a positive way

To learn more about being diplomatic in an email, see Chapter 10 in the companion volume *English for Academic Correspondence*.

4.11 What's the best way to apologize?

Below is a typical apology via email. Note how the email is structured.

> *(1)* I am very sorry for missing our appointment this morning. *(2)* Unfortunately I ... *(3)* I hope this did not inconvenience you. *(4)* I know you are very busy at the moment with examinations, *(5)* but would it be possible to reschedule our appointment to Thursday or Friday this week. *(6)* Once again sorry not to have come and for not having let you know before the meeting was due to start.

Begin by apologizing (1). You can do this in various ways. The examples below go from informal to very formal:

I'm sorry that I missed … I'm sorry for missing …

I am very sorry that I missed … I am very sorry for missing …

I apologize for missing … I apologize that I missed …

Please accept my apologies for missing …

Note the difference in spelling between the verb (*to apologize, she apologizes*) and the noun (*an apology, my apologies*).

Give an excuse (2). Whether you give an excuse or not is up to you. I suggest that you only make genuine excuses (maybe you had some serious family problem to deal with), but don't mention things like your alarm failed to go off, or that you had been up all night partying!

Show empathy (3, 4).

Be flexible in suggesting when to rearrange something (5).

Reiterate your apology (6).

If you want to apologize in advance for something that you will not be able to do in the future you can say:

I'm sorry but I won't be able to make our meeting today.

I am afraid I will not be able to attend class today.

I thought I would just let you know that I won't be able to …

4.12 Is it OK to ask my professor to write me a reference letter/letter of recommendation?

Yes. To learn what procedure to follow with your professor and to see how a reference letter or letter of recommendation should be written, see Chapter 11 in *CVs, Resumes and LinkedIn*, which is part of the Springer series "A Guide to Professional English".

4.13 Should I email my professor to thank them for a course or for helping me in some way?

It is natural for us to enjoy genuine signs of appreciation for our hard work. So, yes.

Here is an example of an email from a female Chinese student to a female professor whose lectures on intellectual property rights (IPR) and intellectual property and communications law (IPCL) the student found very interesting and useful.

Not until I read the news about Apple's lawsuit in China about its trademark (iPad) infringement this morning, did I realize how close IPR is to our daily life and how vital it is for the business strategy.

I'd like to express my thanks to you for the amazing lectures you taught for this semester. In the beginning I knew nothing about the IPCL and studying laws might seem to be boring, however, you made the law vivid and practical. I really enjoyed the lectures although sometimes it killed me to read so much material and I was always under pressure to do those presentations.

Like the saying goes, "what pains us trains us". I learned a lot from the class and began enjoying doing presentations. Moreover, it greatly raised my interest in IPCL for the unique role it plays in business and the vast advantage it could bring if used properly.

The news I read this morning about the lawsuit of the ownership of iPad trademark in China makes me realize the increasing importance of IPR in China where it used to be regarded as the barren land for IP protection. The power IP brings to the Chinese market could be tremendous and revolutionary. I'm very glad and excited about what I learned in this class because it gives me a better understanding and a different perspective. I really hope that my study of IPCL will continue even when the course is over and we will be able to keep in touch.

Thanks again for the wonderful lectures you gave us!

The professor would obviously have been very happy to receive this email i) because it is always nice to be praised, and ii) because it shows that all her (the prof's) hard work was worthwhile.

68

This was the reply the student received from the professor.

> Many thanks for your e-mail. Your very kind words really touched me. It was a great pleasure for me to spend those weeks with you, I wish it hadn't ended so soon.
>
> Of course, we'll try to keep in touch and ... follow my blog!

The student was genuine in her enthusiasm (she was a student of mine too), and by writing such an email she also has the benefit of being able to contact the lecturer again maybe to ask for a reference letter or some kind of recommendation. This may sound opportunistic, but this is how the world works!

Chapter 5

Participating in Lectures, Tutorials, Meetings, Workshops, and Seminars

What the experts say

Meetings are indispensable when you don't want to do anything. John Kenneth Galbraith, US (Canadian-born) administrator & economist

The length of a meeting rises with the square of the number of people present. Eileen Shanahan, US journalist

A workshop is where you do actually get feedback on your work, not just something where you go and sit for a day. Octavia Butler, African-American science fiction writer

One look at an email can rob you of 15 minutes of focus. One call on your cell phone, one tweet, one instant message can destroy your schedule, forcing you to move meetings, or blow off really important things, like love, and friendship. Jacqueline Leo, President and Editor in Chief of The Fiscal Times

Workshops and seminars are basically financial speed dating for clueless people. Douglas Coupland, Canadian novelist and artist

One of the terrific aspects of MIT in those days was the enormous variety of experimental work that either took place there or was talked about in seminars by outside speakers aggressively recruited by the faculty. Robert B. Laughlin, Professor of physics at Stanford University, and Nobel prize winner in 1998

© Springer International Publishing Switzerland 2016
A. Wallwork, *English for Interacting on Campus*,
English for Academic Research, DOI 10.1007/978-3-319-28734-8_5

5.1   What's the buzz?

1) Answer the questions.

1. What, if any, is the difference between a class, meeting, a workshop and a seminar?

2. What meetings, workshops and seminars have you attended since starting your course? Did you enjoy them?

3. Do you think that meetings, workshops and seminars are an effective use of time? What problems stop them from being effective?

4. What kind of preparation can / should you do for classes, meetings, workshops and seminars?

5. In a group meeting among students, should there always be a chairperson? If so, what duties should he / she have?

2) Guess/Choose the answers. Note: the term 'professor' here covers all types of instructors - full professors, lecturers, PhD students doing teaching etc.

1. In a class of 40 students or less, how many students account for 75% of all interactions: a) 20 b) 10 c) 5

2. In a typical class in the US, what percentage of the talking is done by the professor: a) 99% b) 90% c) 80%

3. Who is more likely to ask their professors to give them feedback on the first draft of their papers? a) native speakers b) non native speakers c) no difference

4. Is your level of communication/interaction with your professor outside class likely to increase your level of participation in class? a) yes b) no c) perhaps

5. Do professors and lecturers in Anglo countries tend to expect their students to interact in class more than professors in non-Anglo countries? a) yes b) no c) perhaps

6. Professors should not tell personal stories or reveal personal details about themselves during lectures. a) I agree b) I disagree c) I don't have an opinion on this

7. Professors should not express their political views. a) I agree b) I disagree c) I don't have an opinion on this

8. Success in a class (in terms of later getting good grades) depends mostly on a) the student's effort, b) the professor, c) external factors beyond the student's control

Now check your answers (see end of this section) and discuss the implications, e.g. how important is it for you to actively participate in class by asking questions and making comments (and is it polite?), should professors encourage students to ask questions and challenge ideas during lectures, how frequently do you interact in class (would you like to interact more?) and what factors would encourage you to participate more?

3) Which of the following do you think are good tactics for you to adopt at a class or meeting / seminar / workshop?

   1. Find out as much as you can about the meeting before you go: a) topic b) who will be present (nationality, position in company, age)

   2. Think in advance about exactly what it is you want to discuss then this will enable you to note down any key words and phrases in English that you might need.

   3. Make sure that the other participants are aware of your level of English.

   4. Ensure that no one tries to dominate the discussion.

   5. Don't be afraid to interrupt – make sure you participate actively.

   6. Always listen carefully to what is being said. Often you may subconsciously be projecting your own thoughts onto the speaker, and what the speaker is really saying may be quite different.

   7. Are the participants likely to agree with what you are going to say? If not, think of ways in English to counteract their objections.

   8. Try to sit near to the people who are likely to talk the most, this should enable you to hear better.

   9. If you need time to reflect on what is being said, suggest having a coffee break to enable you to collect your thoughts and prepare what you want to say.

   10. After the meeting, send the chairperson an email summarizing what you think has been the outcome of the meeting.

4) A study group is a group of students who meet regularly in order to study together and at the same time make the experience of assignment and exam preparation less stressful and more enjoyable. Imagine you were going to set up a study group. What ground rules would you need to set?

5) The following exercise is meant for group work only (i.e. not for self study). Discuss what barriers into the research areas below (if any) should be put in scientists' way? What are the consequences of research being and not being blocked?

RESEARCH INTO:	TOTAL BAN	SOME RESTRICTIONS	NO RESTRICTIONS
cloning human beings			
enabling women to give birth at over 60			
more efficient nuclear weapons			
infectious diseases whose results could be used for bioterrorism			
how the human species evolved			

6) Analyse the discussion you had in Point 5. Answer the questions below.

1. How focused and effective was your discussion?

2. Did everybody participate equally or did some people tend to dominate?

3. How important is it for everyone to be able to participate?

4. What strategies can you use to prevent someone from dominating a discussion?

5. What strategies can you use if you are the type of person who talks a little too much in order to enable you to hear the opinion of others?

****

As you will have learned from exercise 2 in the *What's the buzz?* section, if you are studying in an Anglo country such as the US or the UK, your professor is likely to expect you to participate actively in class. This also entails improving your listening skills, pronunciation and your strategies for understanding native speakers - these three factors are covered in Chapters 11, 9 and 10 respectively.

A survey of business executives found that the main causes of ineffectiveness during meetings were: poor preparation, not focusing on the topic of the meeting, participants talking too much (or too little), not listening properly to what other people are saying, and length. Many of those factors are true for meetings, workshops and seminars held at university, and also for classes / lectures.

This chapter is designed to show you how to avoid some of those problems and how to make the most from lectures and all kinds of meetings. The chapter also outlines how to use your English in the most effective way possible, even if your level is not high or when you are in group of native speakers.

Subsections 5.2, 5.3 and 5.4 contain ideas for participating in class and conducting a study group - the examples given are quite informal. However, the example phrases given in the rest of chapter are relatively formal. You might find that native-speaking students use less formal phrases during the meetings, seminars and workshops held at your university amongst students of the same department. However, the idea is for you to learn phrases that you can then use not just with fellow students, but also at workshops at conferences, at meetings that you might be required to go to during internships, and later during your professional career.

KEY TO EX. 2 1) c 2) c 3) a 4) a 5) a 6) research has shown that this is typical of professors of all disciplines in US universities; the idea is to show students that professors are normal people who can be approached, they are not just experts in their field 7) generally speaking it is not considered good practice for a prof to express his/her political views 8) a - normally, but students often attribute their (lack of) success to their professors

5.2   Should I intervene in class? If so, how?

If you are studying in an Anglo country, your professor will probably encourage you to participate by:

1. challenging what he / she has said, i.e. objecting (politely!) to an idea that he/she has put forward - remember that professors may be deliberately provocative in order to encourage their students to react and consequently ask questions

2. asking for further explanations when something is not clear

3. commenting on what a fellow student has said

See 14.6-14.9 for some useful phrases for the above three points.

Professors and lecturers will probably begin their first class / lecture, by telling you if, when and how you can ask questions and make comments. If you are not sure on a particular professor's policy, check with another student. Remember that the prof's basic aim is to encourage you to think critically and not simply accept everything they tell you.

You can improve the way you communicate in class by watching and listening to your fellow students. What you may notice is that

- there is no particular turn taking - you don't have to wait your turn before making a contribution

- students tend not to talk to each other while the professor is talking

- students don't necessarily feel 100% certain about what they are saying - they are not worried about losing face in front of their fellows

- you can interrupt another person - but do so at an appropriate moment, and be polite

- professors will try to give everyone eye contact in order to encourage everyone to talk (rather than the normal four or five students who tend to do most of the talking)

5.3 What are the benefits of interacting and the drawbacks of not interacting?

If you interact you will

- be noticed by your professor. This is a good thing as it will facilitate communication outside class too: the professor will already have an idea about who you are and will probably make more time for you and help you in the future

- show that you have been listening and that you are motivated to learn - again, this will have a positive impression on your prof

- find that communicating in front of an audience (e.g. at a presentation at a conference) is much easier if you are used to having people's eyes on you and being the center of attention

- generally improve relationships with your fellow students - they will know who you are and what your opinions are

If you do NOT interact you will lose all the benefits listed above and moreover your prof may

- think you haven't read or understood the materials needed for the lecture

- feel that you are not interested in the topic or that you have nothing original to say/contribute

If you do not interact because you are shy or are embarrassed about your English, or because you are not used to having in-class discussions, then you could explain this to your prof but assure him / her that i) you will try and overcome your shyness or reticence, ii) you plan to improve your English by attending English courses.

On the other hand, if you have no problems interacting ensure that you don't go to the opposite extreme and interact all the time and dominate discussions - professors don't appreciate these traits either.

5.4   What can I do if I am too shy to participate actively?

You might feel more courageous to participate if you have prepared well for the lesson or meeting (see 5.10).

Another solution is to take part in online course discussions, in which you will:

- have the time to decide exactly what you want to 'say'

- be under no pressure from fellow students or instructors

As a result you may then gain the confidence to speak more during class.

5.5   What is the point of a study / discussion group?
And what is a tutorial?

In some universities in the US and UK, big classes are encouraged to divide themselves up into smaller groups, called a 'study group' or 'discussion group'. The groups may be headed by a student or by a teaching assistant (e.g. a third-year PhD student).

Forming a study group with four or five other students is a way to:

- create closer relationships with other students

- investigate different learning styles

- get feedback on your ideas and brainstorm new ideas

- prepare for exams together

- improve your skills both as a chairperson and participant

- learn and revise in a relaxed environment

- ask for detailed explanations about concepts that you may not have understood in class

The added benefit is that being part of a study group will help you

- to participate better during classes and lectures (see 5.3 and 5.4)

- when you begin working in the 'real' world, e.g. being part of project group, being an effective team member, learning how to be a good chairperson or leader

Unlike a study group or a discussion group a tutorial tends to be run by a professor, with perhaps a higher number of students (5-10), and typically in universities in the UK, Australia and New Zealand. In the UK, a tutorial may also be a one-to-one session with your tutor. In the US, a tutorial generally refers to some online didactic resource.

5.6   What ground rules should a study group have?

If your group is not organized by a teaching assistant, then you should establish:

- when you are going to meet and how often

- how to have discussions - will someone 'chair' the meeting? will it always be the same person?

- decide who will be responsible for what

- set deadlines

- undertake regular progress reviews on how effectively you are working together as a group

Typical phrases you might need are:

So how often do you think we should meet?

What about meeting twice a week?

I reckon we should …

If it's going to work well, I think we need a chairperson.

And maybe we could rotate - one week it's me, next week you etc

I think we should take it turns to be responsible for …

Do we need to set deadlines, and how strict should they be?

5.7 What are the various ways to express opinions during meetings and study groups?

Note that the expressions used in this subsection are quite formal. In a less formal context you might simply spend your time saying: *I think*, *I don't think*, *I agree*, *I don't agree*.

You can express your opinion or make suggestions in two main ways, by:

1) focusing on your own personal viewpoint (using *I*, *me*, *my*)

> It seems to me that ...
>
> As I see it ...
>
> My inclination would be to ...

2) making it sound like a joint opinion (using *we* or no pronoun). This is a more diplomatic approach and leaves the decision more open.

> From a purely scientific point of view, it would make more sense if we ...
>
> Why don't we ..?
>
> What about ...?
>
> It might be a good idea to ...

Even if you use *I*, you can still make the opinion sound less strong and more tentative:

> I wonder if we could ...
>
> I (would) recommend/suggest that we should ...

When a meeting involves people you have not met before, it generally pays to adopt a soft approach. So if you disagree with someone, it is best to avoid direct statements such as *I completely disagree* or *I can't accept that*. Instead, you can use more indirect expressions:

> I'm sorry, but I have reservations about ...
>
> Actually, I'm not sure that that is necessarily the best approach.

Also it helps if you show that you have listened to what another person has said and appreciate its importance from their point of view.

I appreciate your point of view but …

I accept the need for x, however …

I can see why you would wish to do this, nevertheless …

I totally understand what you're saying but …

To learn more useful phases for use in meetings see 14.8 and 14.9.

5.8   I don't want to do group work because it is against some of my cultural values. What should I do?

If you go to university in an Anglo country, this implies that you accept that everyone is treated the same regardless of gender, race, religion, social class, and sexual orientation.

This means that if your professor asks you to work with someone or to set up a study group, you will be expected to do so. Even if working with a particular person or persons would be unacceptable in your own country, in your host country you need to try and accept the different culture.

Your professor is unlikely to show you sympathy if you say to him/her *sorry but I cannot work with this person because* … Your relationships both with your professor and your fellow students will suffer if you continue to adopt any behavior that could be considered as being discriminatory.

Universities in Anglo countries aim not to tolerate any kind of discrimination.

5.9   How can I prepare a summary of what I have been reading / testing for the study group?

Often you will have to do some reading or some lab tests in order to prepare for a discussion in your study group. You will then probably be called on to orally present (with or without slides) what you have studied/tested. A typical structure for what you say could be:

TESTS

The aim of the test was to … Basically I wanted to find out whether … To carry out the test I used … I followed x's methodology … This involved … The main result of the test was … Another interesting result was … What I wasn't expecting was … One of the limitations of the test was that … I think that what the test proved was … I believe this has implications for … What I plan to do next is …

ARTICLES (CHAPTERS, REVIEWS ETC)

The authors of the article are ... The title of the article is ... and in fact it talks about ... The authors claim / sustain / maintain that ... In their opinion ... There are basically three main themes ... They attribute x to y .... They also mention ... They quote from various other articles, including ... What I found the most interesting aspect was ... What I didn't really get / understand was ... They conclude that ... I would (not) recommend reading this article because ...

Note how the 'tests' structure is very similar to an Abstract for a paper, and the 'articles' structure recalls a Review of the Literature. To learn more about these two important sections of a research paper see Chapters 13 (Abstracts) and 15 (Review of the Literature) in the accompanying volume *English for Writing Research Papers*.

If you plan to use slides during class or group activities (e.g. for a panel presentation), then you could also consult *English for Presenting at International Conferences*. While the latter book is intended for conferences, all the guidelines given are also appropriate for informal presentations that take place at your university.

5.10 How should I prepare for a (relatively formal) seminar or workshop?

It has been calculated that 80% of the outcome of a meeting is decided even before it takes place. There are several factors that can contribute to a successful meeting.

- Find out as much as you can about the topic of the meeting before you go and also who will be attending.

- Decide exactly what, if anything, it is you want to discuss, then note down any key words and phrases in English that you might need.

- Prepare a script of anything particularly important that you want / need to say. Then practise reading your script aloud. Modify to make it more concise and convincing.

- Try to predict what people are likely to say. Write down some key phrases that will help you to agree with or counter what they might say.

You should also learn phrases connected with expressing your opinion, interrupting people, disagreeing etc. - see 14.8 and 14.9.

5.11 Is it a good idea to arrive early at a meeting / workshop / seminar?

Not everyone will arrive at the same time. It is a good idea to arrive early. You will then have the opportunity to meet and chat with the other attendees as they arrive. In the case of people you have never met before, this will give you a chance to:

- speak some English in a non-critical situation, i.e. it will not be a problem if you make some mistakes in your English during small talk with other participants

- have an opportunity to hear the voices of the other participants and to tune in to the way they speak

The result will be that you will be less nervous when the meeting starts and you will stand a greater chance of understanding what the other attendees are saying.

5.12 What can I do if the native speakers or fluent speakers dominate the discussion?

Unfortunately, whether deliberately or not, the native speakers (or the most fluent English speakers) may tend to dominate a meeting because of their advanced linguistic skills. This can even lead to unwanted outcomes for the non-native speaking party.

It is critical that you make the native speakers aware of your lower level of English. You can do this in various ways:

1) announcing the fact that your English level is low:

    I am sorry, but my English is not great. Please could you speak slowly and make frequent summaries.

2) apologizing for the fact that you may need to make frequent interruptions

    I would like to apologize in advance if I need to interrupt you to clarify that I have understood.

3) suggesting frequent breaks – such breaks will not only enable you to rest your brain, but also will be an opportunity for you to evaluate about what has been said so far and also discuss it with your colleagues

    Would it be alright to schedule short breaks every 30 minutes? This is because it is very tiring talking for long periods in a foreign language.

4) saying that you and others who speak your language may need to discuss things in your own language

> I hope you don't think it rude if my Spanish-speaking colleagues and I occasionally say something in our own language.

By referring to one or more of the four points above you will be partially able to compensate for your linguistic disadvantage.

5.13   My English is not great. How can I optimize it for the purposes of the meeting?

Below are some general rules about speaking in English during a meeting.

- Make the other members of the meeting aware of your level of knowledge of English, if low, before the meeting starts - this is essential.

- Don't hesitate to ask for repetitions or for the person to speak more slowly (provided that you have made them aware of your level) - the English speaker should be encouraged to remember that the only reason you can't understand is that he / she speaks English and not your language.

- Don't be afraid to interrupt – make sure you participate actively.

- Don't worry too much about grammatical mistakes. It is infinitely preferably to speak fluently and coherently with a lively voice, than with perfectly constructed sentences said in a slow monotone. Try to sound confident even if you aren't.

- Try to improve your intonation. Learn how to show enthusiasm or disapproval. Depending on your mother tongue, your usual intonation might seem rather rude in English or disinterested. If you can't help your intonation, at least make sure your facial expression reflects what you're trying to say.

- Try at least to pronounce the words in your particular field of research correctly with the right stress.

5.14 How can I interrupt someone and what should I do if I am interrupted myself?

Due to your English level, you may not feel sufficiently confident to interrupt some-one else while they are speaking. The secret is to use a combination of body lan-guage (moving forward in your chair and perhaps raising your hand slightly) and to say 'sorry' followed by one of the following:

Could I just say something / interrupt?

Do you mind if I just say something?

I'd just like to ask Luigi a question.

If someone interrupts you and you are OK about this you can say:

Please go ahead.

That's fine, I've said everything I wanted to.

If you wish to continue speaking:

Sorry, if I could just finish what I'm saying …

Can I just finish what I was saying? It will only take me a minute.

If there is an external interruption (e.g. someone has to take a phone call, someone comes into the room, there is a loud noise), to return to what you were saying:

Going back to what I was saying / I said before …

OK, where was I? / What was I going to say?

OK, what we were saying? Oh, yes, I was saying that …

See 14.9 to learn other phrases that you can use when interrupting or being interrupted.

5.15   How can I get silent or shy attendees to talk more?

A seminar or meeting will be much more successful if all attendees express their opinion so that all points of view can be taken into account and a consensus achieved. If you simply say:

Do you all agree on that?

Does anyone have any comments?

What's the general view about that?

you risk that the quieter attendees (or those whose English is poorer than the other attendees) will say nothing even if they might have something useful to contribute. Instead, it is best to ask them by name:

Katsumi, would you like to comment here?

But even the above question may not be effective because Katsumi could simply answer 'no'. So it is best to ask more direct questions.

Katsumi, what do you think would be the advantages of …?

Shigeko, how would your tutor react if we took this decision?

By asking questions that require a specific answer, you ensure that attendees become much more involved in the decision-making process.

5.16   Is it worth making mini summaries?

Whatever your level of English, it is worth checking both for yourself and on behalf of your colleagues, that you have understood what has been discussed and agreed so far. So, after each key has been discussed, you can say:

Can I just check that I have understood what has been decided?

Could someone just summarize for me what has been agreed so far?

5.17 What typical phrases are used to wind up a meeting, seminar or workshop?

Typical phrases that a chairperson will say in order to wind up (conclude) are:

In conclusion …

To sum up …

So, if you'd like me to summarise what we've …

So just to summarize what we've been saying …

If no one has offered to make a summary, you can consider offering to make a summary yourself in order to check that you have understood everything. This will avoid having to clarify misunderstandings at a later date.

Can I just summarize what we have decided, to check that I have understood everything correctly?

So if I have understood correctly, we have decided to …

Other more informal phrases that you might hear at the conclusion of a meeting and which indicate that the speaker thinks that the meeting can be terminated, are:

I think we've covered everything so let's finish here.

I think we can stop here.

Shall we call it a day?

Shall we wind things up?

The meeting process usually does not end with the termination of the physical meeting. There may be follow up tasks. You can ask:

Are there any more seminars scheduled for this project? Do we need to schedule some?

Is there anything I / we should be doing to implement what we learned at this workshop?

Do you want us to / Would you like us to prepare anything for …?

Chapter 6

Listening and Questioning During Lectures

What the British say and what they really mean!

"I hear what you say." = "I disagree and do not want to discuss it any further."

"With the greatest respect …" = "I think you are wrong."

"Correct me if I'm wrong." = "I know I'm right, please don't contradict me."

"Perhaps you would like to think about …" = "This is an order. Do it or be prepared to justify yourself."

"Do as much as you think is justified." = "Do it all."

"It is a pity that you …" = "I am most upset and cross."

"Very interesting." = "I don't agree/I don't believe you."

"Could we consider some other options?" = "I don't like your idea."

"I'll bear it in mind." = "I will do nothing about it."

"Please think about that some more." = "It's a bad idea: don't do it."

"I'm sure it's my fault." = "I know it is your fault, please apologise."

"That is an original point of view." = "You must be mad."

"I'm sure you'll get there eventually." = "You don't stand a chance in hell."

© Springer International Publishing Switzerland 2016   87
A. Wallwork, *English for Interacting on Campus*,
English for Academic Research, DOI 10.1007/978-3-319-28734-8_6

88

6.1 What's the buzz?

The "quotations" on the previous page come from a booklet purportedly written for Dutch executives to enable them to understand the real meaning of certain British English expressions when interacting with British business men and women. Answer the questions below.

1. Do you think the examples are just designed to show the dry British sense of humor or do you think there is some truth in the 'real' versions?
2. Imagine that you had not read the phrases on the previous page. What would you understand if someone said to you: "I hear what you say" or "Very interesting" or "I'm sure it's my fault" or "Could we consider some other options?"
3. Have you met any British people who say one thing and mean another? Do people do anything similar in your country? Do you think people from North America are more straight-talking than the British?
4. If you fail to communicate successfully with a native speaker, do you think it is totally your responsibility?
5. Realistically, what percentage of what a native speaker says do you think you should be able to understand?
6. Do people in different parts of your country always understand each other? How easily do you think native English from different parts of the world understand each other?
7. What strategies can you use to help yourself understand more of what native speakers are saying?
8. Apparently 2 in 5 American graduates think that 40% of the world's population speak English, whereas only 1 in 5 do. What, if any, do you think is the effect of this mistaken belief on the way US students communicate with students from other countries.

****

Dr Sue Fraser, lecturer in English, Seisen Jogakuin College, Japan recommends the following to non-native speakers:

> If you fail to communicate successfully with a native speaker, do not immediately assume it is because of your English ability. Many native speakers are unaware that their spoken English is difficult to understand. This means that they often speak too fast, use inappropriate language (e.g., colloquial structures and expressions), and may also have a strong regional accent that you have probably never been exposed to before. The secret is not to be afraid or embarrassed, but to inform the native English speaker that you are unable to understand.

This chapter is designed to show you why you may have difficulty in understanding native English speakers (e.g. classmates, professors). Knowing why you can't understand may then help you to improve your listening skills.

By improving your listening skills you will then be able to participate more in class, because you will know what questions to ask, what comments to make, and when it is appropriate to interrupt someone else who is talking.

In this chapter you will learn

- the type of questions you can ask during a lecture

- how many native speakers have difficulty understanding each other. For example, someone from Dallas, Texas, might find someone from Newcastle in England totally incomprehensible, and vice versa—simply because they both have strong accents, though they may also use a different vocabulary

- how to recognize key words in English, which tend to be enunciated more clearly, with greater stress and louder volume. By focusing on these key words rather than trying to understand each individual word, you should thus be able to understand the logical flow

- that much of what people say in spontaneous speech is redundant, so there is no need to try to understand each individual word

- how to improve your listening habits

See 14.7 to learn phrases that you can use when you don't understand or need clarification.

6.2 How much you understand also depends on how much you pay attention

A typical lecture in the US or UK will last between 50 and 60 minutes, but you may have a series of two-four lectures in sequence, with only 10 minute breaks between them.

Thus you will be expected to concentrate for long periods at a time. This is not easy even when listening to people speaking your own language.

In fact, studies indicate that the attention span of the average adult is between 15-20 minutes. Obviously it is even harder for you to concentrate for long periods when listening to a foreign language - English.

There are various strategies you can adopt:

- watch the longer presentations from ted.com (see Chapter 2 in *English for Presentations at International Conferences*), take notes as you do so, and then compare your notes with the script. This should help you to improve your powers of prolonged concentration

- some lecturers / professors make their slides available to students - you could ask your prof if you could see the slides before his/her lecture, so that you can familiarize yourself with the topic and possibly prepare questions to ask

- if you can't access the slides, at least find out beforehand as much about the topic as you can - this means learning the meanings and pronunciations of key words so that you are more likely to hear (and recognize them) when the lecturer uses them

- if you interact by asking questions this will keep you more alert - even if you don't ask the questions aloud, you could make mental questions

- record the lecture - but ask permission from the lecturer before doing so. This really only works well with certain lecturers who actually announce which slide they are talking about, otherwise it is very easy to get lost when you are listening to your recording. Lecturers are unlikely to authorize you to do video recordings.

6.3 Note taking

Taking notes may be a good way to lengthen your attention span (see 6.2). However a possible problem is that when writing you may actually miss what the lecturer is saying.

If you do take notes:

- use a txt mssg style to help you write quickly

- use headings

- write in English to avoid your brain having to work on translating

- after the lecture and while the lecture is still fresh in your mind, make sure you can actually read your notes

- compare your notes with a fellow student - this will involve you discussing the content of the lecture together and is an excellent way to discover how much you really understood

- if there is something you don't understand in your notes (in the sense of the content/concept), then ask the lecturer to clarify in the next lecture - lecturers appreciate this as it gives them an opportunity to revise what they did in the previous lecture and to check that students have been following

6.4 Notice how the lecturer uses particular phrases and intonation to give signals

Become familiar with all the little words and phrases that people use when they are moving from point to point, when they are listing things, and when they are summarizing. If you know all these phrases in advance, then you'll be able to follow the lecture itself much better. Typical phrases are:

An example would be …
Some examples are …
The kinds of things that spring to mind are …
So let's move on to …
Another thing to consider is …
Moving on to the next slide …

Note that:

Well that's all I wanted to say about …

To sum up …

So basically what we've been saying is …

In conclusion …

Note than when your professors move onto a new subject or when they want to emphasise something in particular, they will tend to use a slightly higher tone at the beginning of the phrase to mark such transitions or emphasis.

6.5 Learn how to ask questions during a workshop, tutorial, informal lecture

As mentioned in 5.2, Anglo profs tend to encourage their students to be interactive during lectures.

Below is a typical series of interactions between a lecturer (L) and students (S) during a discussion during a lecture. The topic is the effect of global warming on Arctic waters, and what the implications are in terms of international laws on environmental issues.

L	I don't know if you have read today's paper but Canada and Russia have been discussing, or should I say, arguing again about their rights to extract natural resources in the Arctic. And this fits in very nicely to what we were talking about last lecture about ecosustainability. So before we look at the legal debate going on between Canada, Russia and various Nordic countries, let me just find out what you all actually know about the environmental issues.
S1	I've read that a quarter of the world's undiscovered oil and gas resources lies in the Arctic. Is this going to produce even more catastrophic environmental problems?
L	Well I think you could also look at the economic benefits for industry of drilling for oil and gas. Those countries that border the Arctic will definitely have great opportunities. Norway is one of the main owners, so to speak, of the Arctic, and is already the third largest exporter of oil in the world. If they can increase, or at least maintain, their percentage share then some might argue that this will lead to greater stability in terms of supply and possibly prices too.

S2   What about new shipping routes?

L   Yeah, they're forecasting that when the ice melts back some of the existing towns, which are all pretty small and hardly industrialized at all, will actually become huge ports. Massive investments are being made in Churchill for example, which at the moment only has one thousand five hundred inhabitants. The idea is that the routes will be much shorter than some currently used and revenues will also be supplemented by the certain increase in tourism too.

S3   But going back to Haana's question about the environment: aren't we going to be seeing fish move further north on a permanent basis?

L   Yes, we are, and this means that the fish are likely to go from one national border to another. For example, there used to be a species of crab that was caught in Alaska and now it is now being caught in a Russian controlled part of the Arctic.

S4   So are the national borders under the sea clearly defined? I mean do we know who is going to get what? It could make a huge difference to a country's economy.

S5   I still think that the long-term negative impact on the environment will counteract any short-term profits for oil companies. It seems to me that the Arctic is in terrible danger. Don't you think that we ....

L   OK, let me deal with one question at a time. So, first, national borders,
      ...

What the above dialog highlights is that:

i) lecturers in English-speaking countries:

- actively encourage students to participate

- are generally eager to know what their students already know about a topic - this helps them to decide what information to give later in the lecture

ii) students:

- need to prepare for lectures in order to be able to ask questions

- can massively improve their interest (and consequently their listening and oral skills) by participating actively

- pick up on each other's questions (i.e. one student makes a statement/question which another student then refers to, e.g. S3's question refers back to something S1 said)

- may make comments at the same time (e.g. S4 and S5)

6.6   Asking questions during a study group session

In Chapter 5 you learned about study groups. Let's imagine that a student presenter (P) has been talking about the use of language on websites around the world and now other students (S) are interacting. Note that the advantages of asking a series of questions is:

- it keeps you focused - if you don't keep following what has been said, you will lose the thread (i.e. the logical progression of the argument)

- it keeps you interested - the more you are involved in a discussion, the more you will learn and the more you will want to learn even more

As you read the dialog, note how none of the people who ask the questions are trying to take over the conversation from the presenter, and neither are they trying to compete with each other. The aim is a collaborative dialog that benefits everyone and in which knowledge is shared.

S1	Although English has no official status as the language of the Internet, I think you would agree that simply given the vast numbers of people who speak English, that makes it the most suitable language.
P	OK that may be the case in some parts of the world, but not for most people in most third world countries.
S2	Why's that?
P	One of the reasons English is so widely used is because England had so many colonies, the most important being the United States. However, if you come from a country that was once a French, Spanish or Dutch colony, for example, you are more likely to speak the language of that colonial power. This means you'll have to learn English as well which means you may not have time to do other important things.
S3	So what you're saying is that English is actually becoming a barrier to Internet literacy?
P	Yes, but there are other problems with English too.

S3 Such as?

P   Well the first is that English is not equal for everyone.

S4 What do you mean exactly?

P   Well native speakers of English often have a huge advantage over non native speakers. I mean I have read messages posted on social media written by Americans and Brits that I simply couldn't understand. The problem is that native speakers have little idea of how to make themselves understood to non-natives.

S5 So ironically the native speakers are actually the worst communicators. And how much do you think the cultural associations of a language affect how well it can communicate ideas?

P   I think this is an interesting question. The same words and phrases may mean one thing to the native speaker but another to the foreigner, and this is true even with native speakers of the same language. I've met British people who couldn't understand some particular words used by Americans. Also English has borrowed so many words from other languages, but the way these words are used may be completely different. And think of the difficulties of English spelling.

S1 So would you advocate adopting another language?

P   I think we do need a neutral language. But I'm not really sure how to achieve this.

S3 But would you want some kind of artificial language like Esperanto?

P   I don't know. Esperanto is great if you speak a language based on Latin, but pretty useless if you are Japanese for example.

Not all discussions go as smoothly at the ones outlined above and in the previous subsection. When there are several native English speakers involved, for non-natives the experience can be quite frustrating. The rest of this chapter is dedicated to helping you realise that

- it is absolutely normal not to understand a native speaker (they often don't even understand each other)

- understanding why you don't understand will actually help you to understand more

6.7 Accept that you will not, and do not need to, understand everything

When we are learning a foreign language, we tend to think that it is important to understand everything that we hear. But when you are listening to someone talking in your own language, you probably don't listen at 100% and nor do you probably need/wish to.

Thus, an essential rule for improving your understanding of native English speakers is not to expect to understand everything they say. My wife and I are both from Manchester in England. When we watch DVDs of US television series, we watch with subtitles—if we don't have subtitles, we sometimes miss about 20% of what is said. However, even if we don't turn on the subtitles and thus miss 20%, we still understand enough to follow the story.

Understanding enough to follow the plot should be your objective too. By "plot," I mean a conversation in a bar, a formal presentation, a telephone call.

In non-strictly technical / scientific encounters, conversations are often more a means of being together, a socio-cultural event in which relations are established, rather than an opportunity for exchanging information. Most of the time, what is said may be completely irrelevant. Quite often talking is merely an end in itself. When we go out for dinner with friends, the main object is not to glean useful information but simply to bond with the people we are with and to enjoy each other's company.

6.8 Be aware that not understanding a native speaker may have little to do with vocabulary

Below is an extract a transcript of a lecturer talking about cultural differences. When I played the recording to my students, most found it extremely difficult to understand. They said that one of the main causes of this lack of understanding was vocabulary (the other main cause was the speed of the voice).

> I think the British culture is to a degree puritanical which contains aspects of sort of you know carefulness with money and not demonstrating lavishly one's feelings in terms of you know gift giving and things like that and I think you know that that's contrasted with you know possibly with the Italian attitude to family, it being incredibly important and that you know what you have you share with your family and you show your sort of, your love for your family by gift giving. What I mean is that …

As you can see there are very few words (e.g., lavishly = abundantly, generously) that are not of common usage. In reality, the words that my students thought they did not know were actually common words they knew very well but just pronounced in what for them was an alien way.

The key to better understanding is not to focus on each individual word but just on the general meaning. In fact as you see many words add no value at all—he says *you know* five times and *sort of* twice in the space of 90 words, thus representing around 15% of his speech.

Another problem is the total lack of structure in what the speaker is saying. Thus your reason for not understanding a native speaker may have little to do with vocabulary. It will probably be due to their accent. As highlighted in the transcript above, it may also be due to a high level of redundancy in what the speaker says combined with a low level of organization.

6.9   Understand why you don't understand

When you read a text, the punctuation (commas, full stops, capital letters, etc.) helps you to move within a sentence and from one sentence to the next. Brackets, for example, show you that something is an example or of secondary importance. Punctuation also helps you to skim through the text without having to read or understand every single word. You don't really need to read every single word as you can recognize certain patterns and you can often predict what the next phrase is going to say.

A similar process takes place when you listen to someone speaking your native language. You don't need to concentrate on every word they say. Unfortunately, although we can usually quite easily transfer our reading skills from our own language into another, we cannot transfer our listening skills—particularly in the case of the English language. English often sounds like one long flow of sounds and it is difficult to hear the separations between one word and the next.

However, spoken English does follow some regular patterns, and if you can recognize these patterns, it may help you to understand more of what you hear and enable you to understand the general meaning rather than trying to focus on individual words and then getting lost!

In the spoken language, we often begin phrases and project our intonation in a particular way, but then we may abandon what we are saying—even in the middle of a word. Thus, unlike the written language, which generally has some logical sequence, the spoken language often seems to follow no logical track and is therefore more difficult to understand. However, by recognizing the intonation we can get a clearer idea of the "direction" in which the speech is going.

The following is an extract from a conversation between an Indian and an Australian, who both now live in England, talking about how impolite they find the English and how this contrasts with the impression they had before they arrived in England.

> Indian: I was astounded as to how often impolite people were in England, whereas I was always taught that English people were incredibly polite and courteous.
>
> Australian: *Yeah, I, you see* this is what happened to me. I thought, *I thought* because I'm brash or because I'm more confident and *you know* outspoken because that's the way generally Australians are, I thought that I would be the rude person *you know* but I was offended a lot more than I expected to be by people's behavior. I thought *you know* because people *would*, wouldn't say things.
>
> Indian: It's almost *as if*, as if the messages that are sent back to your country and my country are completely different to the reality of *actually* what's going on at the time.

What you can notice is that they don't speak in a logical flow, particularly the Australian. They have not prepared what they are going to say, so they just talk as ideas come into their head. There is a lot of redundancy (highlighted in italics) due to repetitions of words and fillers (*you know*). So they use a lot of words but don't actually say very much in terms of real content.

I think it is extremely important not to focus on every single word and not to think that every word a person says will be important. For example, you might think that the words *brash*, *confident*, and *outspoken* are all key words, but they essentially mean the same thing. Basically, the Australian is saying that he thought the English people might find him a little offensive, but in reality he was the one who was offended.

It is also important to remember what the function of a social exchange is. It is not essentially to exchange useful information, but instead, to create a relationship. At the end of this conversation the Indian and Australian will feel closer to each other because they have shared a common experience or common perception—this is what they will remember; they will not remember necessarily the exact words that each other used to describe this perception. Note also that sharing similar cultural perceptions will generally have a more positive result in terms of the relationship between the speakers, than talking about differences in culture.

6.10 Learn how to recognize key words

When spoken at high speed, English words seem to merge together to create one long noise. For example, the simple question "do you want to go and get something to eat?" when spoken fast becomes "wannagetsomingteat?"

The problem for you and other non-native speakers is that you have probably learned to say the first version in which each word is clearly separated from its neighboring words, and you will therefore be unable to clearly recognize the native version.

So if spoken English is similar to the noise of an express train, how can you possibly understand a native speaker? The key is not to try and differentiate between the sounds and words, but to focus only on those parts of the phrase that are said the loudest and with the most emphasis. When native speakers say *do you want to go and get something to eat*, they don't give each word the same stress and the same volume.

English is what is known as a stress-timed language, which means it has a kind of in-built rhythm that native speakers follow. This may be one of the explanations for the success of rock music and rap sung in English.

The words that are given the most stress are generally those that have the most importance in the phrase: *do you want to go and get something to eat.*

If someone said to you *want get eat* with an intonation that suggested they were asking you a question, you would not have too much difficulty in understanding their meaning. So what you need to try and train yourself to do is just to focus on those words with the most stress. By "stress" I mean a combination of three factors: clarity, volume, and length. Thus, the key words in a phrase tend to be articulated more clearly, at a higher volume, and at a slower speed.

This means that the words that add little value to the phrase are said much less clearly, at a lower volume, and considerably faster. However, given that these words tend not to give key information, you can just ignore them and still have a good chance of understanding the overall meaning of the phrase. Basically, the time it takes to say *eat* will be approximately the same as it take to say *to go and*.

In theory this might sound very logical and even obvious. Of course, in practice it is much harder. However, with some self-training, a more relaxed approach, and more realistic expectations about what you are likely to understand, this method is certainly less stressful than anxiously trying to understand each individual word in a phrase. If you focus on individual words and sounds, you will soon get lost and lose track of the conversation. If, instead, you focus on every fifth or sixth word, i.e., the words that create the rhythm, then you will be more able to keep up with the conversation.

Here is an example from a conversation between an Anglo-Italian, an American, and an Indian talking about the role of the family in their respective countries. The words in the larger font were stressed by the speakers—by 'stress' I mean that the speaker's voice was louder and he/she spent a longer time to say the words. The words in the smaller font were said much more quickly.

Note that if you only understood the words in the larger font, you would still have a general idea of what was said during the conversation. On the other hand, if you tried to concentrate on understanding all the words, you would soon get lost and would be unable to continue participating in the conversation.

> Anglo-Italian: I think in Italy, I mean the family has to take priority, it always has done, I mean that's the kind of core of society and then it kind of unwinds from that, it spirals out from that and I think on the whole they've managed to keep it together through very basic traditions like, for example, the whole sort of ritual of eating together. It's important that at least once a week the whole extended family coming together to fight and scream and laugh and joke or whatever.
>
> American: I wonder if that has something to do with the size. It's interesting to me for instance that because most countries in Europe are much smaller than the North American experience, where family units are closer together. So for instance in North America it's not unusual to have a son or a daughter two thousand miles away in you know New York city, while the family is in Los Angeles, and moving around for economic reasons is just considered normal.
>
> Indian: I think that that happens in India as well but it often depends on where, where you come from, a vast majority of the country is quite poor and the main emphasis is just on existing and surviving and what you say about the family being important is certainly absolutely crucial and key.

Some of the stress words you might still not understand (e.g., *unwinds*, *spiral*, *scream*) but if you only heard the words—*Italy*, *family*, *priority*, *core of society*, *eating*, *extended family*—you would still have an idea of what the Italian was talking about.

6.11   Listen rather than focusing on what you are going to say next

We speak at between 120 and 150 words per minute, but as listeners our brains can process between 400 and 800 words per minute. This means that we get distracted easily and start thinking about other things. If you really want to improve your listening and thus to understand better what other people are saying to you in English, then you need to focus exclusively on what this person is saying. If you start thinking about your next question (or other things), you will quickly get distracted. Try to think at the same speed as your interlocutor rather than being constantly ahead of them.

6.12   Improve your listening habits

American author Robert McCloskey once remarked: *I know that you believe that you understood what you think I said, but I am not sure you realize that what you heard is not what I meant.* People hear what they want to hear.

You can improve your chances of hearing what your interlocutor wants you to hear if you

- focus not just on the first part of what someone says but also on the last part (our tendency is to listen attentively at the beginning and then half listen toward the end)

- participate in a conversation with an open mind, that is, you need to put aside any prejudices you have about, for instance, politics, ethics, and religion - if you listen without prejudice you will hear more of what is actually said rather than what you think is being said

- decide that the topic being discussed is potentially interesting, rather than immediately deciding that it is of no interest to you and thinking about other things

- pay attention, rather than pretending to pay attention

- try not to get distracted by any mannerisms your interlocutor may have

- focus not just on the facts that you are given, but how these facts are given, and what interpretation your interlocutor is giving them

Chapter 7

Successful Conversations and Discussions

What the experts say

The art of conversation is the art of hearing as well as of being heard.

> *William Hazlitt (1778–1830), English writer and grammarian*

It is an impertinent and unreasonable fault in conversation for one man to take up all the discourse.

> *Richard Steele (1672–1729), Irish writer and politician*

Never speak of yourself to others; make them talk about themselves instead: therein lies the whole art of pleasing. Everyone knows it and everyone forgets it.

> *Edmond de Goncourt (1822–1896)*
> *and Jules de Goncourt (1830–1870), French writers*

Encounters with people of so many different kinds and on so many different psychological levels have been for me incomparably more important than fragmentary conversations with celebrities. The finest and most significant conversations of my life were anonymous.

> *Carl Jung (1875–1961) Swiss psychiatrist,*
> *founder of analytical psychology*

Apart from theology and sex there is really nothing to talk about.

> *Harold J Laski (1893–1950), English political scientist*

Beware of the conversationalist who adds "in other words." He is merely starting afresh.

> *Robert Morley (1908–1992), English actor*

When Arabs meet their countrymen for the first time, they usually attempt to establish each other's family identity. In the West, on the other hand, it appears that the initial conversation revolves around a person's occupation or profession. In Japan, introductions are made with reference to one's organization or company.

> *Farid A Muna, chairman of Chairman*
> *at Meirc Training and Consulting*

© Springer International Publishing Switzerland 2016
A. Wallwork, *English for Interacting on Campus*,
English for Academic Research, DOI 10.1007/978-3-319-28734-8_7

7.1 What's the buzz?

1) What makes a conversation successful between two people who have just met? How should the participants behave and react to each other? What should they <u>not</u> do?

2) The dialog below is an example of what in many countries would be considered as an unsuccessful conversation. It is between a Japanese (female) and a *Lithuanian* (male) student who have never met before. They are waiting for the first lecture to start at a course they have both enrolled on.

Sorry, is this seat taken?

No.

There are a lot of people here for this lecture, aren't there?

Yes, there seem to be.

Have you done any lectures with this professor before?

Yes.

Hi, my name's Eriko Suzuki, I am Japanese. And you?

I'm from Lithuania.

Where exactly is Lithuania?

Near Latvia.

I see. How are you finding life in this university.

OK.

I really like the informal atmosphere and the friendly profs. And you?

Yes

Oh, I have just seen a friend of mine over there. Bye.

The dialog is obviously exaggerated, but it does highlight a common problem in conversations—ones that are completely one-sided. The Japanese woman is trying to be friendly, but the Lithuanian rejects all her attempts at getting the conversation going. It may simply be that the Lithuanian is shy and / or is worried about not speaking good English. But the impression the Lithuanian gives to the Japanese woman is that he simply does not wish to communicate. This leads to a breakdown in the communication and the result is that the Lithuanian misses a possible opportunity to get to know another student from another culture and possibly learn about some similar research to his own.

3) Below is a different version of the same dialog. How is it different? What strategies do the speakers use to keep the conversation going and show interest in each other?

Sorry, is this seat taken?

No sorry I just put my bag here that's all. I'll just move it so you can sit down.

Thanks. There are a lot of people here for this lecture, aren't there?

Yes, the professor is supposed to be really good.

Yeah, I have read a lot of her papers. Really excellent. Where are you from?

From Lithuania. And you?

I am from Tokyo. I'm Eriko, by the way.

Henrikas. Good to meet you.

Excuse my ignorance, but where exactly is Lithuania?

It borders with Russia in the west, so it's in Europe. So you were saying you are from Tokyo, do you mean you were born there?

4) Now compare your answers to Exercise 1 with the bullet points below. In a successful conversation (i.e. Exercise 3), the two people:

- immediately start a friendly conversation

- share experiences

- show interest in what the other person is saying

- repeat back the same question that they have been asked

- repeat back what their interlocutor has just said to encourage him / her to continue

- avoid dominating the conversation and take equal responsibility for its success

- interrupt a lull (i.e. a silent pause) in the conversation by referring back to what the other said earlier

The keys to a successful conversation are as follows:

- take equal responsibility for keeping the conversation going

- introduce new topics naturally—don't jump from one topic to another

- link what you say to what the other person has just said

- show interest

- provide relevant information (e.g. the fact that Lithuania borders with Russia and is in Europe is much more useful than saying that Lithuania is next to Latvia, which is another small country that a Japanese person might not be familiar with)

******

To have a successful conversation and consequently to improve your chances at being involved in new research collaborations, you need to learn a series of social skills. These include being able to break the ice, carry forward a conversation, listen carefully, create an interpersonal bond, take turns in talking, collaborate with your interlocutor to fill silences by referring back to something that was said earlier, react sensitively to what is being said, contribute and make the right comments / noises when someone is telling a story, embark on safe topics, and exit when required. When speaking in another language, we tend to forget the social skills that we have in our own language. However, these skills are imperative for successful academic and social encounters.

In this chapter you will learn how to

- show interest in your interlocutor

- make small talk and have informal discussions

- improve your listening skills by taking a more active part in conversations and by perceiving listening as a productive rather than passive activity

- involving everyone in the conversation

- directing the conversation to areas where you have better vocabulary / grammar

For useful phrases to use in the context of socializing see 14.11.

7.2 I am too shy and embarrassed to have a conversation in English, what can I do?

One common reason for an unsuccessful conversation between two people is that one of the people fails to contribute to the conversation because they are too embarrassed about their level of English or because they don't talk much even in their native language.

Do you like standing up in front of other people or do you feel nervous and self conscious? If you are the kind of person who usually does not talk much at dinners, parties and even in everyday banal social situations (e.g. in front of the coffee machine, on the telephone), then try and make an effort to talk more and find yourself at the center of attention.

Other ways to become used to being the center of attention or at least to have people focus on you include:

- joining a dance or acting group

- offering to do presentations at work

- talking to strangers sitting next to you on trains and planes

- sports coaching for children

- doing voluntary work

Don't just listen to people, learn to have the courage to interrupt them and comment on what they have said. For instance you can relate what they have said to your own experience. You could say:

I know exactly what you mean. In fact …
Actually I had a very similar experience to what you have just described.
I was once in exactly the same situation.
I completely agree with what you are saying. In fact, …
I am not sure I totally agree with you. In my country, for instance, …

Tell people things that have happened to you or that you have read or heard about. You can do this in low risk situations (i.e. where your conversation skills and level of English are not going to be judged), for example, when you are with a group of friends.

You could practise doing two-minute presentations with a group of other students. You could either do this in your own language or in English. Possible topics:

- what you enjoy doing most in life

- your favorite movie or book and why you like it so much

- the worst journey of your life

- the best holiday

- your dreams for the future

If you practice being at the center of attention you will gain more confidence.

7.3 Begin by making small talk

Small talk means the initial exchanges people have on non-risk topics such as the weather, your accommodation and flat mates, lectures you have attended, and professors whose courses you are following.

Such exchanges enable you and your interlocutor to

- get used to each other's accents and style of speaking. You are not giving each other essential information, so it does not matter at this point if you do not understand everything you say to each other

- find your voice in English

- make a connection with each other

- learn a little personal information that you might be able to refer to in future conversations

- make some positive comments about each other. This will help you cement your relationships with fellow students

Typical questions that people ask while making small talk are as follows:

It's a bit cloudy, isn't it?
Do you think it's going to rain later on?
Yesterday's course was good wasn't it?
The profs all seem OK don't you think?

To move the conversation forward, you can introduce yourself. This gives you an easy way to begin talking about life at the university and the various courses.

By the way, my name's ...

What course are you on?

Are you living here on campus?

Which year are you in?

How are you finding it so far?

7.4   Show interest

Everyone likes it when people show genuine interest in them—it gives them a feeling of importance and recognition. You can show interest in other people by asking questions and by showing that you are 100% focused on listening to the answers. If you find a topic that seems to interest your interlocutor (i.e. the person you are taking to) more than other topics, then try to ask more questions about this particular topic. In any case, focus on questions that you think that your interlocutor will take pleasure in answering.

If you are not naturally curious about other people, a good way to think of questions is to use *how*, *where*, *why*, *when*, *what*. For example:

How did you find out about this course?

Where are you living?

Why did you choose this particular university?

When does the course on x begin, do you happen to know?

What will we be studying?

When you listen to the answers, try to show some reaction or at least that you are listening to what your interlocutor is saying. The most typical word native speakers use is *really* which is said in the form of a question and is designed to encourage the speaker to continue. Another typical comment is *right*.

For example, let's imagine that you are at a social dinner at a conference taking place in Budapest (Hungary).

So where are you from?

From Stockholm in Sweden.

Oh right, so how did you get here?

By train.

Really?

Yes, I don't like traveling by plane.

Right.

And you, where are you from?

Well, I'm from Budapest actually.

Oh really?

Yes, I was born here.

Other expressions you might use are

I see.

That's interesting.

Wow.

Fantastic.

It might feel very unnatural for you to use any of these phrases, but remember you should not say them in an exaggerated way with a lot of emphasis. Just say them in a neutral way and quite quietly. They are basically verbal noises that demonstrate to your interlocutors that you are interested in what they are saying.

7.5 Ask open questions

Some questions could simply be answered *yes* or *no*. For instance:

Did you have a good time at the party last night?

How was the lecture this morning?

The above questions are called closed questions, because potentially the person could simply answer *yes* or *no* and thus "close" the conversation. Typically, they make use of auxiliary verbs (*did, can, are, have*, etc.). If you find that your interlocutor is just giving you *yes no* answers, it will soon become an effort for you to continue the conversation. So you could rephrase the questions as follows:

So, what was the party like? How long did you stay? Who was there?

What exactly was the topic of this morning's lecture? How much did I miss?

The above are what is known as open questions, and again they make use of question words such as *what, which, why, when, where*.

7.6 Ask follow-up questions

The natural course of a conversation should not be a series of unrelated questions and topics, but a thread of logically linked questions. First you ask a topic question and then you ask another question (or make a comment) related to the same topic in which you ask for more details. Here is an example:

You: So where did you go on holiday this summer?

Them: To Berlin.

You: (1) *Follow-up*: So what did you think of the architecture?

You: (2) *Comment*: I've heard the architecture is amazing.

You: (3) *Encouragement*: So tell me all about Berlin.

7.7 Encourage your interlocutor to continue talking on the same topic

There are many ways to encourage someone to give more details on a topic that has just been initiated:

Restate part of what they have just said:

Them: But the food was terrible.

You: Terrible?

Them: Yes, in fact we had one really bad experience when …

Make mini summaries of what they've just said:

You: So the architecture was great, but the food was terrible.

Them: Yeah, and then we had a few problems at the hotel.

Paraphrase or agree with what they just said:

Them: Exactly. And his presentation was so boring.

You: (1) *Agree*: Yeah, really boring.

You: (2) *Paraphrase*: Yeah, a complete waste of time. <u>I thought that the only interesting part was</u> …

Show interest by asking for clarification:

> Them: And the hotel was not exactly cheap.
>
> You: What do you mean by "not exactly cheap"?
>
> Them: Well they added on a lot of extra services.
>
> You: For example? What kind of services?
>
> Them: And they had a disco every night.
>
> You: So you're saying that it was very noisy? You didn't get much sleep. <u>I had a similar experience last month in</u> …

Note how in the above exchanges the strategy is to use the clarification to initiate something that you want to say, i.e. the underlined phrases above. Basically you are showing respect for the other person by using a clarification to show interest in what they have said. This then allows you to take your "speaking turn" in the conversation. If you ask for clarification this also enables your interlocutor to make any adjustments to what they said either to help you understand better or to add details.

People sometimes announce that they have done something. They then generally expect you to make a comment on it so that they will be encouraged to give you more details. The examples below are not connected to each other:

> Them: I saw a fantastic movie at the cinema last night. You: Oh really what was it called?
>
> Them: My sister has just started university. You: Oh yes, so what is she studying?
>
> Them: I have just come back from New York. You: New York. Fantastic. What were you doing there?

You also need to be able to respond to comments (rather than questions) that are directed at you.

> Them: You're lucky to have an airport so close to your university.
>
> You: Yes, it's very convenient especially with all the traveling I have to do.
>
> Them: The weather should be good when you get back home.
>
> You: Yes, summer's in my country tend to be dry and not too hot.

7.8 Make "announcements" rather than asking all the questions

If you find that you are asking all the questions, then there are two possible results. One is that you may become frustrated with the attention always being focused on your interlocutor. The other is that your interlocutor might think that you are being rather invasive.

So sometimes you need to initiate a topic yourself. If for example you have been asking question's about your interlocutor's hotel (as in 7.7 above), you can announce:

You: Well unlike you, I am staying off campus in the main town.

You: I actually went to Munich last year. I don't know how it compares with Berlin, but …

In the above examples you have directly related your experience to your interlocutor's experience. You also show that you have been listening carefully as you have repeated some of their concepts and phrases.

Other times you may want to initiate a completely new topic.

This afternoon I am giving a presentation.

Yesterday I had a look around the old town.

Tonight a group of people from my department are going to …

By introducing a new topic you hope that your interlocutor will ask you some questions, and thus create a more balanced exchange. However, bear in mind that if your interlocutor seems unwilling to contribute it may have nothing to do with you—they may just be having a bad day.

7.9 Avoid dominating the conversation

Many non-native speakers are afraid or embarrassed about not being able to follow a conversation due to poor listening skills. One strategy that some use is to try to increase the amount of time they spend speaking. Clearly the more you speak, the less you need to understand other people.

If you adopt this "talking rather than listening" strategy, continually check that your listeners are following you and are interested in what you are saying. If they are not giving you any eye contact, it probably means that either they cannot understand you or they have lost interest.

Below are two tactics for taking the focus off yourself.

Transfer their original question back to them:

> Them: So, are you going anywhere interesting this summer?
>
> You: blah blah blah. And what about you? Have you got any plans for the summer?

Ask them if they have had a similar experience:

> You: .. and during the presentation my laptop suddenly crashed.
>
> Them: Oh no!
>
> You: So I had to blah blah blah. Have you ever had any disasters like that?

7.10 Feel free to interrupt people who talk too much

In 1711, Joseph Addison, English essayist, poet, playwright, and politician, wrote,

> The English delight in Silence more than any other European Nation, if the Remarks which are made on us by Foreigners are true. Our Discourse is not kept up in Conversation, but falls into more Pauses and Intervals than in our Neighbouring Countries. To favor our Natural Taciturnity, when we are obliged to utter our Thoughts, we do it in the shortest way we are able.

Not everyone delights in silence! Some people are used to talking a lot and having a quiet audience. For you as a listener, in a social context this may not be too much of a problem. You can simply "switch off," look out of the window, and start thinking about something more interesting. However, when having a discussion about your research - informal or formal - you may wish to get your own point of view across. In such situations it is perfectly legitimate to interrupt. You can say in a friendly tone:

> Sorry to interrupt you but …
>
> Can I just make a point?
>
> Just a minute, before I forget …

7.11   Involve everyone in the conversation

There is often a tendency in a group conversation for those who speak the best English to dominate the conversation and to form a sub group. This leaves the rest of your group in silence. If your English is at a higher level than some of the others, or if you are more extrovert than them, don't use this entirely to your own advantage or as an opportunity to show off your excellent English in front of your colleagues. Instead people will appreciate it if you try and involve them. Here are some examples of how to do draw people into a conversation:

Vladimir, I think you have had a similar experience haven't you?

Monique, you were telling me earlier that …

Bogdan, I think you and Monique must have the same tutor.

Kim, Melanie told me you are into bungee jumping.

7.12   Avoid long silences

Different cultures have different tolerance levels for the length of periods of silence in a conversation. So don't think that you necessarily have to fill every silence. You can use the pause to think up new areas that you could talk about. Below are some tactics for re-initiating a conversation.

Return to a topic mentioned earlier or other information that you know about the person:

So you were saying before that you had just come back from a conference. What exactly was the conference?

I seem to remember that you did a Master's in sports psychology, am I right?

Introduce a new topic:

So did you go to the party last night?

Did you hear about that hurricane in Florida?

So do you think Germany will win the world cup?

7.13   Prepare for the social conversations at formal occasions

During your time as a student you will probably also attend more formal functions, such as social dinners at conferences.

You will probably be able to participate more effectively in a conversation if you initiate the topic area yourself. You could prepare short anecdotes on one or more of the following:

- travel stories (e.g. missing planes, terrible hotels)

- the worst presentation you ever did

- the best / worst conference you ever attended

- the best / worst professor you have ever had

These are good topics because they are neutral and everyone in your group is likely to have something to contribute. If you initiate the conversation, it will help to boost your confidence.

An alternative to stories / anecdotes are factoids (i.e. interesting statistics), for example factoids about your country, about your research area, or about anything you find interesting.

It is also helpful to learn something about psychology and communication skills. Socializing is all about relating to people and communicating well with the other attendees. Learning good communication skills and social skills entails knowing how the human brain receives information, and how we perceive each other.

If you are asked a question, try to move the conversation forward by giving some extra information in your answer. For example, if someone asks you, "So are you a student here?" you could say, "Yes, I am a PhD student. I'm actually doing research on how people who vote for right-wing parties have a very narrow world view." If you just replied "yes" then your questioner might perceive you as either being rude or reluctant to continue the conversation.

7.14 Direct the conversation to areas where you have a wider vocabulary or knowledge

Sometimes your ability to participate in and contribute to a conversation will depend on the vocabulary you have available on that particular topic. If you feel you don't have the vocabulary required, you could try to gently shift the conversation to an area where you know a greater number of relevant words. Of course, this shift must be to a related area rather than a totally new topic, unless there is a complete silence where it would be justified to change topic.

Food is often a subject at social dinners, regarding not only the menu of the meal itself, but also discussions about the national and typical dishes of those around the table. Discussing such dishes involves a lot of specialized vocabulary regarding ingredients and cooking techniques. However, there are other aspects of food that also have a strong cultural interest. You can inject considerable interest into a conversation about food, if you talk about the social aspects of food and eating, rather than just typical dishes. For example, you could discuss

- taboos—what foods are not acceptable to be eaten by humans (e.g., in the UK, horsemeat is rarely eaten, and cat and dog meat are never eaten)

- fasting—what foods are prohibited for religious reasons at certain times of the year

- events—what foods people eat on particular occasions (e.g., in the USA it is common to eat turkey to celebrate Christmas)

- etiquette—how guests are expected to behave (e.g., can you refuse if your host offers you more food? should you take a gift, if so what is and is not appropriate? should you take off your shoes before entering someone's house?)

- production methods—e.g., genetic modifications

- the pros and cons of being vegetarian

- food allergies

There are three ways to do this:

- Wait for a pause in the conversation and initiate a change in topic by saying: *In my country at this time of year, we can't eat meat …*

- Invite others to begin a discussion by saying: *I am curious to know whether anyone else is allergic to …*

- Ask a question: *In your country do you have many vegetarians?*

The result of this is that you will find social events more rewarding and less frustrating.

7.15   Bear in mind cultural differences

It is very important to bear cultural differences in mind. For example, there are many differences between the way the English and the Chinese interact with each other socially. The English say "I am sorry" or "Excuse me" very frequently, when they inadvertently touch someone, sneeze, or stop someone in the street to ask for directions. To a Chinese person such constant apologizing seems excessive. On the other hand, the Chinese are more likely to express their concern about someone's health by recommending, for example, that the person should wear more clothes or drink more water. To an English person, such suggestions may seem too personal or inappropriate.

7.16 Use conversations to practise your English grammar

If you are keen to improve your English, then you could try directing the conversation so that it covers a particular topic that involves a grammar point you want to practise. For example, imagine you want practise in using future forms (in italics below). You could start off new conversations by asking questions such as:

Do you think there *will be* more technological changes in the next decade than there have been in this decade?

How do you think climate change *is going to affect* your country in the next few years?

By 2040 *will we all be speaking* Chinese?

By 2020 *will we have solved* the problem of world debt?

Or you could ask more personal questions

Where *are you planning* to go for your next holiday?

What a*re you going to do* immediately after this lesson?

Do you think *you'll survive* this PhD course?

Are you going to watch TV tonight?

Will you be going to Steve's party on Friday night?

Note how in the example questions many different forms of the future have been used: will, going to, present continuous, future continuous and future perfect.

Chapter 8

Telephoning

Factoids: 200 years of telephony

1876 First words spoken on a telephone

1877 First phone sold

1880 London's first phone directory (255 names)

1889 First coin pay phone

1901 First transatlantic wireless message

1922 First fax

1933 First speaking clock

1949 First answering machine (initially called the *Electronic Secretary*)

1960 First fully automated mobile phone system for vehicles

1983 First cordless phone sold

1984 One of the first videoconferencing systems sold

1989 First satellite telephone service

1999 First full Internet service on mobile phones

2000 Turkish inventor markets a phone with a built-in lie detector

2003 First Skype call made (originally called Sky peer-to-peer, then Skyper, and finally Skype)

2007 First iPhone sold

2009 Google Voice launched

2014 Microsoft Mobile launched

2050 First interplanetary home-use telephone network

2076 Fault-free telepathy replaces need for telephones of any kind

© Springer International Publishing Switzerland 2016
A. Wallwork, *English for Interacting on Campus*,
English for Academic Research, DOI 10.1007/978-3-319-28734-8_8

8.1 What's the buzz?

1) Answer the questions.

1. How do you say telephone numbers in your language? Does it follow the same formula as you've heard native English speakers using?
2. What do you say when you answer the phone?
3. How are telephone directories organized in your country? Do you ever use either paper or online directories?

2) Discuss the two quotations below. To what extent do they apply (or could they apply) to your life as a student?

Whatever your field, you will create a strong impression when you communicate by phone; this can be either good or bad, and may well last. It is thus critical to prepare for any important telephone calls in advance, so that your listener will grasp the reason for your call immediately and will be motivated not just to listen, but to act on any request you may make. Telephone communication is not as straightforward as it may seem, and the fact that we cannot see facial reactions and that misunderstandings may more easily arise and be more difficult to resolve must always be born in mind.

If you have something important to say to someone with whom you have never previously had contact, then use the phone rather than email. Through an initial phone call people become real to each other. This sets up a positive relationship which can then be continued via email. On the other hand, a rushed email may contain errors and create the wrong first impression. People pay more attention to a phone call than they do to email. Future communication will be more successful, if you start the relationship in a positive manner.

****

This chapter covers how to make formal telephone calls, for example the kind of language you would need to phone professors, a fellow researcher in an important project, administrative people at your university, or institutes or companies where you are planning to do an internship.

Thus the kinds of calls you might make to fellow students are not covered here. However, if you are interested in learning some typical words used in text messages and chats, or if you want to know all the varieties of smileys, then see Chapter 13.

In this chapter you will learn how to

- decide whether and when to phone your professor

- make formal phone calls

- plan in order to make the call more effective

- react when you don't understand your interlocutor

- conclude the call

Note that in all the example dialogs in this chapter, the part spoken by the student is in normal script, and the part spoken by the admin person is in italics.

See 14.14 to learn phrases for use on the telephone.

8.2   Decide whether another form of communication might be more suitable

Most professors will prefer to be contacted via email rather than phone as it allows them to deal with your request in their own time.

You should really only phone your professors when there is absolutely no other solution, for example, if there has been a major misunderstanding between you and there is no opportunity for you to meet face to face, or if you have some kind of technical emergency that needs resolving immediately.

However, bear in mind that phone calls are possibly the most difficult form of communication in English for non-native speakers. Also, think about how your professor might react to your phone call - will it be at a convenient time for him/her? Will he/she be able to give you a quick answer to your question?

So first of all consider whether your phone call is really necessary, and whether it wouldn't be simpler for you, or at least for your counterpart, simply to send an email.

8.3 Prepare and practice

The level of success of your phone call can be enhanced considerably if you have a very clear idea of what you want to say before you actually make the call. Write down some notes about what you want to say, and then make sure you know how to say everything in English.

If you are planning to call someone who you have not already met it is useful to find out something about them. Is this person a man or a woman, old or young? What level of formality will you have to use? What is their level of English? Are they a native speaker? Have any of your fellow students spoken to this person? What can you learn from their experience: for example, does this person have a reputation for speaking very fast? If so, you need to learn appropriate phrases for encouraging them to slow down.

Think about what the other person might ask you, and prepare answers to such questions. If you do so, you are more likely to be able to understand the question when it is asked.

If you have an important call to make, you may find it useful if you simulate the call with another student, and ask the student to ask you pertinent questions.

8.4 Consider using an email as a preliminary information exchange before the call

The more both parties are prepared for a telephone call, the more likely the call will be successful. If you have a call that will require a complex discussion (e.g. to discuss a paper that you are writing for a conference with a researcher in another county), it is not a bad idea to send each other a list of points that you wish to discuss. This will enable you to

- think about what you need to say and how to say it

- think about what useful phrases in English you may need

- tick the items from the list as you discuss them, and make notes next to each item

You could suggest such an email exchange by writing:

Before we make our call I thought it might be useful to send you this list of items that I would like to discuss. If you have any additions I would be glad to receive them. Then it would be great if you could give me a few hours to look through them. Thank you.

8.5 Think about the time and the place of the call

Some people find that the quality of their English is also affected by the time of day, the level of stress they are under, and their location. Try to analyze at what point of the day your English seems to work best. Choose a place to make your call where you will have minimal external interference.

You may find it easier to speak in English when your colleagues are not listening to you, so you will feel less inhibited.

8.6 Beware of ringing people on their mobile phone

You are unlikely to have the person's full attention if you call them on their mobile: you may well be disturbing them in the middle of something else. It is generally a good idea to ask:

Is this a good time or are you in the middle of something?

Am I interrupting something?

If they then say *Well, actually I am with someone at the moment. But go ahead, what can I do for you?* it is probably best to call back later:

Sorry, I have obviously got you at an inconvenient time. What time do you think I could call you back?

8.7 Help the person that you want to speak to

The person you wish to speak to may not be expecting your call. When they receive your call, they will probably be in the middle of something else and need a few seconds to reorient themselves. To help them

- say your first and second names (the switchboard operator may not have given your correct name to your interlocutor)

- explain the context—that is, the relevant communication you've had with this person, for example, *you may remember that I sent you a document two weeks ago, well I am calling because …*

- explain why you are calling

If they don't understand what you are saying and you are speaking reasonably slowly, it may simply be that they don't understand a particular word or phrase. Try and rephrase what you've said, instead of repeating what you've said before.

8.8 Learn the structure and typical phrases of a telephone message

Often the person you wish to talk to may not be available. The following examples are designed to show you the language used in a typical telephone conversation, where one party leaves a message.

EXAMPLE ONE

Department of Engineering. Good afternoon can I help you?

Could I speak to Professor Alvarez please.

I'm afraid Professor Alvarez is not in her room at the moment, I think she's just gone out to lunch.

Do you know what time she will back?

Well she normally takes about half an hour. Shall I get her to call you as soon as she comes back?

Actually could you possibly give me her mobile number. It's quite urgent.

I am really sorry but I am not authorized to.

Is there any chance of you ringing her for me and asking her to call me back?

Certainly, I can do that for you. Could I have your name please.

Yes it's Estefania Dalgarno.

Sorry what was your surname again?

Dalgarno. d a l g a r n o

OK Estefania I'll ring her straight away. Goodbye.

EXAMPLE TWO

Department of Engineering. Good afternoon can I help you?

Yes, this is Andrea Baumann from the University of Munich. Could I speak to Professor Yang please?

Sorry I didn't catch your name, could you speak up a bit please the line's bad.

Yes, it's Andrea Baumann.

And where did you say you are ringing from?

The University of Munich.

OK, I'll try and connect you. … Sorry, the line's busy. Do you want to leave a message?

Could you tell her that Andrea Baumann called, and that I would like to post-pone the tutorial meeting till next Tuesday.

That's Tuesday the seventh right?

Right. But if she needs to speak to me she can get me on 0049 that's the code for Germany, then 89 656 2343. Extension fifteen.

That's one five right?

That's it.

Can I read that back to you to make sure I've got everything?

Sure.

Andrea Baumann, that's B-A-U-M-A-N from the ...

No, two Ns, M-A-double N.

OK, from the University of Munich. You want to postpone the tutorial meeting till Tuesday the seventh, and she can reach you on 0049 89 656 2334

Sorry that should be four three, not three four.

OK 2343, extension 15, one five.

That's it. Thanks very much. Bye.

Goodbye.

8.9   Practice spelling out addresses

Being able to spell out your email address without confusing your listener is a key skill when participating in a telephone call. This is because if communication between you and your interlocutor is difficult or impossible due to language diffi-culties, the easiest solution is to continue the communication via email. To be able to continue via email, at least one of you needs to give their email address. In reality you increase your chances of continuing the communication if you both give your addresses. Here is an example dialogue of someone giving their email address:

My address is anna_southern at virgilio dot it. That's anna A-N-N-A under-score ...

Sorry, what is after ANNA?

Underscore.

Underscore?

The little line between two words.

OK.

So, underscore then Southern. That's S as in Spain, O, U, T as in Turkey, H, E, R, N.

Is that N as in Norway?

Yes, that's right. Then at virgilio dot it. That's V, I, R, G, I, L, I, O dot I, T.

OK. I'll just repeat that. anna that's with two Ns right?

Yes, A double N A.

Then underscore S, O, U, T, H, E, R, N. So annasouthern, that's all one word, right?

Yes, that's right-

Then at virgilio, that's V, I ...

If your address is rather complicated (e.g., with an underscore, slashes, or very long), it is not a bad idea to have a personal email address that is short and which is simple to say, which you can use for emergencies!

Here is an example dialogue of someone giving their website address:

So it's www englishconferences forward slash R1256 dot pdf.

Sorry does englishconferences have a dot between the two words?

No it's all one word.

Then forward slash. The letter R. Then the numbers 1, 2, 5, 6 as digits not as words. Then dot pdf. Have you got that?

I'll just read it back to you. So, that's forward slash ...

Below is an example of how to dictate the following traditional postal address over the phone: Adrian Wallwork, Via Murolavoro 17, 56127 Pisa, Italy

Adrian Wallwork. That's a-d-r-i-a-n new word w-a-l-l-w-o-r-k. New line. Via Murolavoro. That's v-i-a new word m-u-r-o-l-a-v-o-r-o, number 17, that's one-seven. New line, 56127 Pisa. New line, Italy.

8.10   When spelling out telephone numbers, read each digit individually

Every language seems to have its own system of reading out telephone numbers, and conventions differ even within the same country. The simplest system is to read each digit individually. Thus to say 113 4345, you would begin by saying *one one three* rather than *one hundred thirteen*.

When reading out landline numbers, it is generally best to separate the country code from the rest of the number. Below is an example of how to spell out 0044 161 980 416 71.

> zero zero four four—that's the code for England—one six one; nine eight zero; four one six; seven one

Note that some people say *oh* rather than *zero*.

Whether you are dictating or noting down an address or phone number, make sure you repeat them at least twice. Even people who speak the same language often make mistakes with numbers.

8.11   Compensate for lack of body language

Unless you are using Skype (or equivalent), the other person will not be able to see the reaction on your face, or whether you are nodding in agreement or not. You can compensate for this by using one of the following expressions: *I see, yes, OK, right* or noises such as *a-huh* and *mmm*. Using such expressions also shows your interlocutor that you are still on the phone and are absorbing the information being given to you. This is extremely important when making phone calls with the Japanese, who expect to hear a constant flow of listening signals.

8.12   Avoid being too direct

When on the phone, you lose a substantial part of your communicative power because the other person cannot see the expression on your face, nor can they read your body language. This is even more true of email (where vocal clues are also lost), but even on the phone it is worth trying to make an extra effort to be polite and diplomatic. If you use very direct language, you may be in danger of sounding rather rude.

The second column in the table below shows some "softer" versions of the phrases in the first column.

POSSIBLY TOO DIRECT	SOFTER
Why didn't you send me the application form earlier?	I was wondering why I hadn't received the application form earlier.
You were supposed to be sending me a form to fill in.	Sorry but I was expecting to receive a form to fill in.
I need confirmation of my accommodation by tomorrow.	I was wondering if you could send me confirmation of my accommodation by tomorrow. Would it be possible by the end of the morning? Do you think you could send me the confirmation by lunchtime today?
I'm calling you about ...	The reason I'm calling you is ...

What you will notice from the "softer" versions is that they require more words and more complex grammar (e.g., use of conditionals, and the past continuous and past perfect). Even if your English is low level, you could simply learn the phrases as if they were idioms rather than as grammatical constructions.

8.13   Use messaging, headphones and speaker phone to aid your communication

You can massively increase the amount you understand by not limiting your conversation to a simple voice exchange. Instead, write messages (particularly of addresses, numbers).

If you are finding it hard to follow what the other person is saying, you can say:

Do you think you could message me what you've just said?

Could you write down the spelling of that name please?

Could you upload a picture or image so that I can visualize better what you mean?

You can understand much more of what your interlocutor says if you wear head-phones. This also frees up your hands for writing messages.

For particular important calls where you are worried you might not understand, consider having a friend to sit next to you to help you understand. You can either use two sets of headphones or put the call on speaker phone. If you use the speaker phone function, remember to mute if you need to talk with the friend sitting next to you.

8.14   Learn how to check that you have understood

The following telephone conversation takes place between a student and an admin person at the student's department. It highlights phrases you can use to indicate exactly what part of the admin person has said that you didn't understand. For more on what to do when you don't understand see Chapter 9, in particular 9.4.

I am sorry could you speak up a bit, I can't hear you very well.

Sorry, is that better? I was saying that you would need to speak to the student accommodation officer.

To the 'what' officer, sorry.

The accommodation officer.

OK, could you give me the name of the officer please.

It's Sarah Milsom.

Sorry I didn't catch the last name.

Milsom, that's M-I-L-S-O-M. Her number is 020 8347 1254.

1254

But before you phone Sarah you need to download the list of flats available. Are you looking for yourself or for other students as well? And you'll also need to tell her what range of price you're prepared to pay.

Sorry I didn't get what you said in the middle, what about other students?

etc etc etc

OK. So can I just summarize the main points of what we've said? So, first ...

Keep checking that you have understood what is being said, and make summaries of your understanding so that your interlocutor can check whether you have correctly interpreted what he / she has said.

If you take notes during the call, it will help you to paraphrase what the other person has said so that you can check your understanding.

8.15 If you really can't understand, learn a way to close the call

There will be occasions when you simply cannot understand. Rather than panicking and putting the phone down with no explanation you can say:

- *I am afraid the line is really bad. I will try calling back later.* You can then prepare yourself better for the next time you call, or alternatively ask a colleague to make the phone call for you

- *I think it might be better just to send an email. I will do this as soon as possible.* You can summarize what you think you have understood in the email, and then ask for clarifications

8.16 Follow up with an email

You and your interlocutor may remember little more than 10% of what was said during your call. Even if you think the phone call has gone well and that you have understood everything, it is always good practice to send your interlocutor an email summarizing the main points. This allows the interlocutor to check his / her understanding of the call as well. In addition, you can ask any questions or clarify points that you forgot to make during the call itself.

Chapter 9

What to Say When You Don't Understand What Someone Has Said

Factoids

❖ Around a billion people travel across borders every year. Around 75% travel from a non-English speaking country to another non-English speaking, yet communicate in English while they are there.

❖ Non-native English-speakers now outnumber native ones 3 to 1. There are more Chinese children studying English—about 100 million—than there are Britons. Around two billion people study English, and three billion people speak it. Eighty percent of the electronically stored information in the world is in English.

❖ Probably the biggest selling book in English language teaching history is Raymond Murphy's *English Grammar in Use*, first published in 1985 and subsequently making its author a multi-millionaire.

❖ Nearly one-third of the citizens of the USA feel that it is not too important or not important at all to speak a second language. The number of children and students studying languages in the UK has dropped considerably, and less money is being invested in language research. Apparently, this lack of language skills has led to a lack of interpreters and is making it harder for international anti-terrorism squads, for example, to work together.

❖ Misunderstandings are as common with people who share the same language as they are in exchanges between people who are talking in a second language. A study in the UK revealed that as many as 6 out of 10 conversations in the workplace lead to a significant degree of misunderstanding.

❖ Native speakers often listen at only 25% of their potential. The other 75% is made up of ignoring, or forgetting, distorting, or misunderstanding what the other person has said. Concentration rises above 25% if the interlocutor thinks what he / she is hearing is important or interesting. But in any case it never reaches 100%.

© Springer International Publishing Switzerland 2016
A. Wallwork, *English for Interacting on Campus*,
English for Academic Research, DOI 10.1007/978-3-319-28734-8_9

9.1 What's the buzz?

1) Discuss the questions.

   1. What makes native and non native speakers difficult to understand? Is what makes a non-native difficult to understand the same as what makes a native speaker difficult to understand?

   2. Who is more likely to say the following - a native or non-native English speaker? What effect does this have on the listener? What can you do as a listener to improve your understanding?

     OK everyone. So I'm gonna start with Freud's concept of dreams. It's kinda like Freud was saying that our dreams are like a mirror of our inner self, you know, that we, that our superego unconsciously expresses itself, I mean, it's all symbolic language and it's all about a disguised fulfillment of a, of a, of a, repressed wish and stuff.

   3. What steps can you take to improve your understanding of native speakers? Discuss at least three strategies.

2) Who tends to perform the best in the following activities – men or women? Or is there no difference (equal)? Do you think the better performance is due to biological characteristics or to social conditioning?

	ACTIVITY	MEN	WOMEN	EQUAL
1	asking for directions when lost			
2	writing diplomatic emails			
3	speed at writing text messages			
4	verbal reasoning & learning languages			
5	finding things (e.g. clothes, food in fridge)			
6	parking a car			
7	buying a car			
8	singing in tune			
9	multitasking (doing several activities at the same time)			
10	cooking			

3) Now read this conversation between a man (normal script) and a woman (italics). Underline the phrases that they each use to indicate that they a) haven't understood, b) need clarification c) are checking that they have understood correctly.

So which ones do you think women are better at?

Well to start with, women are much better than men at finding things.

Much better at what sorry?

Finding things. It's because our range of vision is much wider, often 180 degrees. We can also see colors much better - ten times more men than women can't tell the difference between red and green. Another reason is that men have more of a tunnel vision which is why tasks such as reading a map are performed better by men, another example is parking a car.

Or buying a car.

Buying a car? Actually no. Studies have shown that women generally get a better deal, they get the price down from a car salesman far more effectively than men do.

So you're saying that if I want a new car I should take my girlfriend along with me?

Exactly. These days more and more cars are being bought by women, 42% in fact, which is a rise of thirteen per cent in the last five years alone.

Did you say thirteen, one three, or thirty?

Thirteen, one three.

Wow! So, what else are women better at?

Women can hear better than men, a woman's brain has been programmed to hear a baby cry at night. And because of that they can hear any emotional changes in children's and adults' voices, their ears are obviously more tuned in to sound in general. In fact, for every man that can sing in tune there are eight women who can do it.

Sorry, 'tuned in'?

What I mean is women are more aware, more conscious of sounds.

What about text messaging? I've noticed that women are so much faster then men.

That's right women tend to be better at anything that involves fast nimble, manual activity.

So is there anything apart from parking cars that men are good at?

Sorry, what did you say?

I was asking if there is anything that men are good at.

Well, most of the world's top cooks are men.

****

Many of my students say they have a feeling of inferiority and inadequacy when they are talking to native speakers. They feel nervous. They feel stupid. They feel that they cannot participate on an equal level.

Native speakers do not always understand each other. As Oscar Wilde noted, "We have really everything in common with America nowadays, except, of course, the language." And another Irish playwright George Bernard Shaw once said, "England and America are two countries separated by a common language."

I am from Manchester (England) and frequently in my life I have had experiences when I fail to understand another native English speaker. I once spent 20 minutes in a taxi in Glasgow (Scotland) in which the taxi driver chatted away to me in a strong Glaswegian accent, and I understood absolutely nothing. When I am in London, I am often unable to understand a single word in the first 30 seconds of what a native Londoner says to me because they speak so fast.

In the English language world we accept that often we do not understand each other.

The solution for you as a non-native speaker is to change perspective. Think about situations within your own country. Presumably there are people in your country who speak with a very different accent from yours, and may even use a slightly different vocabulary or dialect. If you do not understand what they say, I imagine that you do not feel any sense of inferiority—at the most you might feel a little embarrassed. In any case, you probably collaborate with each other to understand what you are saying.

So when you have to speak to native speakers, try to imagine that English is simply a rather obscure dialect of your own language! Your objective and that of your interlocutor's is to understand each other. You should both be on an equal level.

In this chapter you will learn how to

- interrupt your interlocutor and ask for clarification without losing face

- identify for the interlocutor exactly what part of their sentence you did not understand

- find a way to help your native-English-speaking interlocutor be sensitive to the fact communication is a two-way process, in which both parties are responsible for helping each other understand. It is thus perfectly acceptable, and indeed often essential, to interrupt your interlocutor, and you shouldn't be afraid or embarrassed to do so

Often when you don't understand what someone says or writes, it has no other consequences than embarrassment and frustration. However, on some occasions, for example, in interviews and technical meetings, it may be crucial to understand all the key points. In such cases it is imperative that you ensure that you are able to follow at the least the main points of what is being said.

This chapter will show you ways to improve your understanding of native speakers and to transform a potentially frustrating exchange into a positive collaboration. The strategies I outline are those that native speakers use with each other all day and every day in the native-English-speaking world. They are not strategies that I have specifically designed for non-native speakers. This means that a native speaker will be very familiar with them, and therefore you do not need to be afraid to use them.

For useful phrases on this topic see 14.7.

9.2   Raise awareness in your interlocutor of your difficulty in understanding

A key factor in your ability to understand native speakers is letting them know that you are not a native speaker and thus your command of the language is not the same as theirs. The problem with a lot of people whose first language is English is that they often don't learn languages themselves. They thus have no idea of the difficulties that you might experience in trying to understand them (particularly if they sound like the person talking about Freud in the first exercise of the *What's the buzz?* section above).

Also they are not aware that you might, for instance, have a good command of spoken English and written English, but that your listening skills are much lower.

If you don't encourage the native speaker to speak clearly, then you will significantly reduce your understanding of what they say. This is certainly not a benefit for you, and is probably not helpful for them either.

Instead you need to make it immediately clear to the native speaker that you need him or her to speak slowly and clearly, make frequent mini summaries, and be prepared for many interruptions for clarification on your part. You could say something like this:

> It would be great if you could speak really slowly and clearly, as my English listening skills are not very good. Thank you. And also please do not be offended if I frequently ask you for clarifications.

But the problem does not end there. Even if the native speaker acknowledges your difficulties, they are likely to forget these difficulties within two or three minutes, as they then become absorbed by what they are saying. This means that you frequently have to remind them to speak more slowly.

> I am sorry, but please could you speak more slowly.

9.3 Identify the part of the phrase that you did not understand

Avoid saying "repeat please" if you don't understand what someone has said. Instead it is much more beneficial for both you and your interlocutor if you precisely identify what part of the phrase you didn't understand. Let's imagine that the part in italics in the sentences in the first column in the table on the next page is the part said by your interlocutor that you did not understand. Your questions for clarification are shown in the second column.

YOUR INTERLOCUTOR SAYS THIS:	TO CLARIFY, YOU SAY THIS:
I thought the presentation was *amazing*.	You thought the presentation was *what* sorry?
	Sorry, *what* did you think the presentation was?
I made *a terrible mess* with my presentation.	You made *a what* sorry?
	Sorry, *what* did you do with your presentation?
We have all just come back from *the trip to the mosque*.	You have all come back from *where* sorry?
	Where did you go, sorry?
I have just had an interesting conversation with Professor Suzuki.	With Professor *who* sorry.
	Sorry, who did you speak to?

In the examples above, I have given two possible clarification questions. For example:

I *thought the presentation was* amazing.

Type 1) You *thought the presentation was* what sorry?

Type 2) Sorry, *what* did you think the presentation was?

Type 1 is easy to use because you simply repeat the words immediately preceding the word that you didn't understand (in the example the repeated words are shown in italics).

Type 2 is more complex because it entails using an auxiliary verb (*did* in the example). It also means that you have to remember to put the words in a question form.

So it is simpler to use Type 1, which you can further reduce to *the presentation was what?*

Both Types 1 and 2 have the advantage that your interlocutor will only repeat the word that you didn't understand (*amazing* in this case). This means that you now have a far greater chance of actually hearing the word, as it will now be isolated from its surrounding words. If you don't understand the meaning you can simply say *Sorry what does that mean?* Or simply repeat the word with a rising intonation to indicate that you don't understand: *amazing, sorry?*

Obviously, you can only use this strategy of repeating words if you hear the words in the first place. And this is another reason why it is very important to listen carefully.

The examples given in the table on the next page are useful when you are focusing not just on an individual word but on a whole sequence of words. If you don't identify the precise part of the sentence, your interlocutor will just repeat everything probably exactly as before, but perhaps a bit louder. By identifying the part you did not understand, there is a chance that the interlocutor will use different words and say that particular part more slowly. The second column also shows alternative forms of clarification.

WORD / S MISUNDERSTOOD	CLARIFICATION QUESTION
It chucked it down yesterday so I couldn't summon up the courage to venture out.	Sorry, I didn't understand the *first part* of what you said.
	Sorry *what* did it do yesterday?
It chucked it down yesterday so I couldn't *summon up the courage* to venture out.	Sorry, I missed the part in the *middle*.
	Sorry *what* couldn't you do?
It chucked it down yesterday so I couldn't summon up the courage to *venture out*.	Sorry, I didn't catch the *last part*.
	Sorry, I didn't understand *the bit after* "courage".
Note: The sentence means: It was raining very hard yesterday and I didn't feel like going outside.	Sorry, I didn't understand *what* you didn't have the courage to do.
	The courage to do *what*, sorry?

9.4 Identify the key word that you did not understand

Here is an extract from a telephone conversation. It highlights the strategies that a non-native-English-speaking woman uses to identify what the native-speaking man has said.

1. Man   Could you tell her that the seminar has been put off until next Thursday.
2. Woman The seminar has been what sorry?
3. Man   It's been put off until next Thursday.
4. Woman Sorry, "put off?"
5. Man   Postponed. It has been postponed till next Thursday.
6. Woman So it's been delayed, but not canceled?
7. Man   Yes, that's right.

The key problem in the above dialog was that the woman did not know the term *put off*. The first time the man says *put off* (line 1), the woman probably hears the following sound: *zbinputofftil*, that is, one long sound where several words have been merged together. Basically, she has no idea what the man said between *seminar* and *next Thursday*. So her tactic is to say all the words she heard until the point where she stopped understanding (line 2). The man then simply repeats the second part of his initial sentence (line 3), but this time probably with more emphasis on *put off*. Because the man puts more emphasis on *put off*, the woman is now able to identify the part of the sentence that she had failed to identify before.

Note how in line 4 the woman begins her sentence with *sorry*. If she had simply said "Put off?" the man might have just answered "Yes, put off" as he would think she was just asking for confirmation. Instead the word *sorry* tells the man that the woman is not familiar with the term *put off*. *Sorry* is very frequently used by native speakers when asking for clarification.

The man now uses a synonym for *put off* (postponed). The woman's final strategy (line 6) is to check, using her own words, that she has understood correctly the meaning of *postponed*. And finally in line 7, the man confirms that she has understood.

9.5 Avoid confusion between similar sounding words

Some words sound very similar to each other and are frequently confused even by native speakers. Below are some examples of how to clarify certain pairs of words.

WORDS	POSSIBLE MISUNDERSTANDING	CLARIFICATION
Tuesday vs Thursday	We have scheduled the meeting for Tuesday.	That's Tuesday the sixth right?
13 vs 30	We need thirty copies.	That's thirty, three zero, right?
can vs can't	I can come to the meeting	So you are saying that you <u>are</u> able to come to the meeting?
	I can't come to the presentation	So you mean that you are <u>not</u> able to attend the presentation?
		So you mean that you <u>cannot</u> attend?

In the first example, the secret is to combine the day of the week with its related date. This means that your interlocutor has two opportunities to verify that you have understood correctly. If you have misunderstood, your interlocutor can then say *No, Thursday the eighth.*

The confusion in the second example happens with numbers from 13 to 19 and 30, 40, 50, etc. Using the correct stress can help: thir<u>teen</u> vs <u>thir</u>ty. However, particularly on the telephone, this subtle difference in pronunciation may not be heard. So the secret is to say the number as a word (e.g., *one hundred and fourteen*) and then to divide it up into digits (*that's one one four*). If you have misunderstood, your interlocutor can then say *No, thirteen, one three.*

In the third example, the problem is increased if *can* is followed by a verb that begins with the letter T. Thus, understanding the difference between *I can tell you* and *I can't tell you* is very difficult. There are also significant differences between the way native speakers pronounce the word *can't*—for example, in my pronunciation *can't* rhymes with *aren't*, but for others the vowel sound of "a" is the same as in *and*. The solution is to replace *can* and *can't* with the verb *to be able to*. You also need to stress the *are* in the affirmative version, and the *not* in the negative version, as illustrated in the table. If you have misunderstood, your interlocutor can then say *No, I am able to come* or *no, I am not able to come* (alternatively *I cannot attend*).

9.6 Turn your misunderstanding into something positive

One way to understand more of what your interlocutor says is to make frequent short summaries of what your interlocutor tells you. Your interlocutor will appreciate the interest you are showing. You can use phrases such as the following to begin your summary:

Can I just clarify what I think you are saying? You mean that …

I just want to check that I am following you correctly. So you are saying that …

Your listener will not interpret such clarifications as a lack of English comprehension skills on your part, but that like a native speaker you simply want an accurate understanding of what has been said.

Using this tactic means that you could turn a potentially embarrassing situation into something positive.

Chapter 10

Improving Your Pronunciation

Factoids

❖ In some research by Dr Sue Fraser, some Japanese high school students were asked to rate their difficulty of listening to and understanding the English of certain native speakers, of a Taiwanese speaker, and of their fellow Japanese. Fraser found that 95% of the students found the Japanese speaker "easy to understand," 52% the Taiwanese, 38% the American, 31% the Scottish person, 18% the English person, and 12% the person from Zimbabwe (where English is the official language).

❖ W.W. Skeat, a professor at Cambridge University, once declared, "I hold firmly to the belief … that no-one can tell how to pronounce an English word unless he has at some time or other heard it."

❖ Some parents in South Korea used to force their children to have painful tongue surgery in order to give them perfect pronunciation, for example to enable them to pronounce 'l' and 'r' sounds. The operation involves snipping the thin tissue under the tongue to make it longer and supposedly more nimble. It became so common that the Korean government produced a film to shock parents into shunning the practice.

❖ British and American pronunciation differ considerably, particularly with regard to vowels sounds, for example: route = *root* (GB), *raut* (US). British people tend to pronounce the second *t* in *twenty*, unlike many North Americans who say *twenny*. The stress within a word may also be different: *detail*, *frustrated* (GB), *detail*, *frustrated* (US).

❖ The vast majority of English surnames have the stress on the first syllable, for example, Babbage, Berners-Lee, Darwin, Dawkins, Faraday, Hawking, Newton, Turing. British towns also have the stress on the first syllable, for example, Birmingham, Cambridge, London, Manchester, Newcastle, Oxford.

© Springer International Publishing Switzerland 2016
A. Wallwork, *English for Interacting on Campus*,
English for Academic Research, DOI 10.1007/978-3-319-28734-8_10

10.1   What's the buzz?

1) Discuss these questions.

   1 What sounds in your own language do non-native speakers find difficult?

   2 What sounds do speakers of your language typically find difficult in English? Why?

   3 In English, can the same word be pronounced in more than one way, depending on its position in the phrase?

   4 Do you find that when you do an English listening exercise in class, or when you watch something without subtitles, that you understand maybe less than 50%, but that when you look at the script or subtitles, you realize you didn't hear or understand even some very easy words? Why do you think this is?

2) Decide which of the following pairs of words rhyme with each other (i.e. the part in italics in both words sounds exactly the same)? Mark them S (the same) or D (different).

   1 lang*uage* / sand*wich*

   2 sl*ow* / th*ough*

   3 man*age* / fr*idge*

   4 *where* / *wear*

   5 ch*ose* / wh*ose*

   6 pr*ice* / pr*ize*

   7 degr*ees* / pl*ease*

   8 *course* / *cause*

   9 *bin* / *been*

   10 *come* / *sum*

3) Mark the stress of each pair of words (as in the example). Mark them S (the same) or D (different).

   1 psy<u>cho</u>logy psycho<u>log</u>ical D

   2 color / colorful

   3 complexity / complex

   4 impulse / impulsive

   5 science / scientific

   6 secret / secretive

7 simplicity / simple

8 sophistication / sophisticated

9 technique / technical

10 unease / uneasy

4) Decide which one word in each phrase would likely be stressed the most.

    a) So you are saying that it is important.

    b) Could you say that last bit again?

    c) Sorry I didn't catch that.

    d) Sorry what is the name of the professor?

    e) I really don't understand what you are getting at.

****

Although grammar mistakes will rarely cause breakdowns in communication, problems with pronunciation sometimes do. It is thus imperative that you improve your pronunciation if you wish to understand and be understood by a native English speaker or other non-native speakers who are not part of your language group.

In this chapter you will learn that

- your listening skills will improve dramatically if you improve your pronunciation

- even though English pronunciation seems quite random, there are a few basic rules

This chapter gives some very general guidelines on word stress (e.g., *manager* rather than *manager*), but there are many exceptions to the guidelines. To learn more about pronunciation and intonation, see Chapter 14 in the companion volume *English for Presentations at International Conferences*.

KEYS

2) all the same except 4, 6, 8 and 9

3) psy**chol**ogy / psycho**log**ical *(D)*, **col**or / **col**orful *(S)*, com**plex**ity / **com**plex *(S)*, **im**pulse / im**pul**sive *(D)*, **sci**ence / scien**tif**ic *(D)*, **se**cret / **se**cretive *(S)*, sim**plic**ity / **sim**ple *(D)*, sophisti**ca**tion / so**phis**ticated *(D)*, tech**nique** / **tech**nical *(D)*, un**ease** / un**eas**y *(S)*

4) a) is b) last c) catch d) what 5) getting

    Ex in 10.5 1) coming, PhD, genetic 2) plan, firstly 3) fifteen 4) please feel free, whenever, don't 5) anyone 6) still, again 7) double, highest 8) let's move on 9) important 10) once, hope

10.2   Avoid the typical pronunciation mistakes of people who speak your language

The first factoid at the beginning of this chapter highlights that

- if you are a non-native speaker, you will find the English spoken by people of your own native language easiest to understand and to imitate

- speakers of languages within the same language group (e.g., Japanese and Chinese; Italian and Spanish) generally understand each other's English relatively easily

- there are big differences in levels of understanding of the varieties of English spoken by native speakers

So just because your colleagues in your own country can understand your English, it certainly does not mean that people from other countries will understand you. For example, if you are from Japan, a Bulgarian may have difficulty understanding your English and likewise you may not understand his / her English.

10.3   Learn what to say if other students tease you because of your English accent

It is generally a good policy to laugh with the people who are teasing you, in that way they lose most of the power that they have over you. In addition, but not as an alternative, you could say:

Hey guys, try and say these words from my language.

With a bit of luck, they will understand the difficulty that you may experience with their language by noticing how difficult your language is.

10.4   Check for the pronunciation of key words in your field

Most of this subsection is lifted from 14.4 of the companion volume *English for Presentations at International Conferences*, where you can find more details about improving your pronunciation.

It is a good idea to write a list of words that you think you may need in a formal occasion, for example a seminar, workshop or conference. In any case, you should certainly learn the correct pronunciation of the key words in your field of research. Here are some online resources:

http://www.howjsay.com (British English)

http://www.learnersdictionary.com (US English)

http://oaadonline.oxfordlearnersdictionaries.com (US English)

http://www.wordreference.com/ (US English)

By using such online resources you can:

- note down where the stress falls on multi-syllable words (e.g. *control* not *control*)

- listen for vowel sounds, and learn for example that *bird* rhymes with *word* and so has a different sound from *beard*

- understand which words you cannot pronounce.

This means that you can find synonyms for non-key words and thus replace words that are difficult to pronounce with words that are easier. For example, you can replace

- a multi-syllable word like *innovative* with a monosyllable word like *new*

- a word with a difficult consonant sound like *usually* or *thesis*, with a word that does not contain that sound like *often*, *paper*

- a word with a difficult vowel sound like *worldwide* with a word that has an easier vowel sound like *globally*

- make a list of words that you find difficult to pronounce but which you cannot replace with other words, typically because they are key technical words

- understand which sentences are too long or would be difficult for you to say

The sounds you have in your own language will certainly influence the sounds that you can and cannot produce in English.

To find out the English sounds that people of your language have difficulty with you can do an Internet search: "name of your language + English pronunciation + typical mistakes." If possible, find a site that (1) lists the typical sounds, (2) has audio (so that you can hear the sounds), and (3) illustrates the shape that your lips and tongue need to make to produce the relevant sound. If you don't have your lips and tongue in the right position, it will be impossible for you to reproduce the correct sound.

10.5   Sentence stress

Generally you should stress the word that carries the key information or that helps to distinguish one thing from something else. This means that normally we stress adjectives rather than their nouns:

I am a philosophy *student.*

You would only stress the noun if it is the noun that helps to differentiate between two things.

I am a philosophy student *not a full-time researcher.*

Stress verbs rather than pronouns:

I want to show *you.*

Only stress the pronoun when you want to differentiate one group of things or people from another.

I want to show you *not* them.

Stress the main verb rather than an affirmative auxiliary, unless you want to give special emphasis.

This has happened *several times.*
I can assure you that this has *happened several times.*

Stress the negative auxiliary rather than main verb (first example below), unless you are distinguishing between two verbs (second example).

This hasn't *happened before.*

I haven't spoken *to him but I have* seen *him.*

Below is a quick exercise to check whether you have understood the concepts above. Look at these phrases from a workshop. Which one word of the words in *italics* do you think will be given the most stress? Are there any cases where all the words will be given equal stress?

1. Good morning, thanks very much for *coming here today*. My name is Haana Magreb and I *am a Phd student* in *genetic engineering*.
2. This is *what I plan* to do today. *Firstly we're going* to look at ..
3. The presentation should last *about fifteen minutes. Please feel free* to ask me questions *whenever you want* and if I use any terms that *you don't understand* please let me know.
4. Have you all got the handout *I sent you* via email?
5. *Does anyone have* any questions at this point?
6. Sorry, *I still don't understand* - would you mind asking me the *question again* in the break?
7. In this diagram, *double circles* mean that this item has the *highest priority*, whereas single circles mean low priority.
8. OK, so that's all I wanted to say about ... Now *let's move on* to some more new developments.
9. OK, we're very close to the end now, but there are just a couple of *important things* that I still want to tell you.
10. Well that brings me to the end of the presentation. *Once again*, thanks for coming – *I hope* it has been useful.

The answers are at the bottom of 10.1.

10.6 Using the correct stress and intonation during a meeting, seminar, workshop etc

When participating in a meeting, workshop, seminar etc, it is essential that you make your point clearly. One way to do achieve this is to stress the key words.

Stressing a word means giving it more emphasis than the surrounding words. You stress a word by saying it a little bit louder and longer than the other words.

Most often the stress words are verbs and nouns, as these generally carry the most meaning. This is illustrated in the example phrases below, in which the chairperson of a meeting is checking the opinions of the participants. The words to stress are in italics

Do you all *agree* on that?

Does anyone have any *comments*?

What are your feelings about the *abstract*?

What are your *views* on this?

If you put the stress on words (pronouns) such as *you, my, his, she*, or on names of people, rather than on the verb or noun, this indicates that you are trying to contrast the views of two (or more) different people.

I understand what *you're* saying, but I am not clear what *Martin's* point is.

I don't think that's for *us* to decide, surely it's for them to *decide*.

Sorry, I meant *your* project not *her* project.

In other cases, if you put the stress on the pronoun you might confuse your listener. For instance compare:

That's not what Martin *meant*.

That's not what *Martin* meant.

In the first case, the speaker is saying that we have not understand the meaning of what Martin was trying to tell us. In the second case, the speaker is making a contrast between what Martin meant and what some other person meant.

Sometimes you will need to stress the adjective or adverb

You may be *right*, but *personally* I …

I'm not sure whether that's *feasible*.

I don't want to sound *discouraging* but …

Am I making myself *clear*?

This needs to be done *efficiently*.

To express what you think is the right thing to do, or to make a proposal sound more tentative, then you would probably want to stress modal verbs such as *must, should, may,* and *might*.

It *might* be a good idea to hear what the prof has to say about this.

Yes, we *should* check with the administrative secretary first.

This *must* be done before the end of the semester.

You *may* be right, but I think there's a strong possibility that …

If you want to give special emphasis to a verb, you can place the auxiliary (*do, does*) before it, and stress that auxiliary. In the examples below the speaker is underlining the fact that she has understood and appreciated the other person's point of view, but that she has some reservations.

I *do* understand what you are saying, but …

What you are saying *does* make sense, however …

Very occasionally, you will need to stress a preposition. However, with prepositions the stress is normally very slight.

Are you *with* me? (= are you following what I am saying?)

Can we do that *before* the break, rather than *after* the break?

In summary, stressing particular words in a sentence:

- helps the listener understand the key points of what you are saying

- helps you to make differentiations (e.g. between different people, different approaches)

- stops your speech from being monotonous

10.7   Word stress

A good simple guideline is that if you have a doubt about the pronunciation of a two-syllable word that is not a verb, then put the stress on the first syllable. In fact, the vast majority of British surnames and place names have the stress on the first syllable. Examples: *Thatcher, Newton, London, Bristol.*

This is not the case of many US names as these have been more influenced by Native American languages, Spanish, and the languages of the settlers.

Some words change stress depending on whether they are nouns (on first syllable) or verbs (on second syllable):

> *contact, exploit, increase, insert, object, present, progress, record, report, research, upse*t.

Apart from those words, if a word can be both a verb and a noun I don't think there is any way of knowing where the stress will be.

The following words are stressed on the first syllable, both if they are a noun or a verb:

> *answer, access, archive, comment, contact, discount, issue, invoice, measure, promise, profit, question, schedule, survey*

The following words are stressed on the second syllable, both if they are a noun or a verb:

> *address, command, concern, control, correct, debate, effect, reply, report, request, respect, result, return, support*

Some words are stressed differently by different people, for example, *research*—some people say *research* and other *research*, irrespectively of whether it is a noun or verb.

A word that is made up of two words has the stress on the first syllable (e.g., *software*). Here are some examples:

> *boyfriend, everyone, feedback, headline, highlight, income, input, interface, interview, layout, newspaper, outcome, overview, podcast, sidetrack, supermarket, switchboard, workshop*

Exceptions: *afternoon, understand*

THREE SYLLABLE WORDS

Most three-syllable words (nouns, verbs, and adjectives) that don't have a suffix (e.g., *un-*, *pre-*) have the stress on the first or second syllable. Only a few have the stress on the third syllable (e.g., *expertise, introduce, Japanese, personnel*).

The following three-syllable words are stressed on the first syllable:

absolute, agency, alias, apparent, architect, article, atmosphere, attitude, bicycle, company, conference, confident, consequence, deficit, difficult, excellent, hierarchy, industry, influence, interested, interesting, modify, monitor, paragraph, personal, prejudice, premises, principle, quality, satellite, sufficient, triangle

The following three-syllable words are stressed on the second syllable:

acceptance, accompany, advantage, assistant, component, configure, consultant, convenient, determine, develop, dishonest, embarrass, example, explicit, financial, ideal, important, objective, percentage, performance, strategic, sufficient

MULTI-SYLLABLE WORDS

Words ending with *-able*, *-ary*, *-ise*, *-ize*, *-yse*, *-ure* have the stress on the first syllable:

suitable, secretary, category, realize, analyze, organize, recognize, architecture, literature

Words ending with *-ate*, *-ical*, *-ity*, *-ment*, *-ology* have the stress on the third to last syllable

graduate, immediate, separate, logical, reality, feasibility, management, development, government, environment, psychology

Some exceptions (stress on second syllable): *equipment, fulfillment*

Words ending with *-ial*, *-ic*, *-cian*, *-sion*, *-tion* have the stress on the penultimate syllable:

appearance, artificial, specific, expensive, politician, occasion, specialisation

Most words ending in *-ee* have the stress on *-ee*.

attendee, employee, interviewee, referee

An exception (stress on second syllable): *committee*

154

The majority of other multi-syllable words have the stress on the second syllable (e.g., *identify, particular, parameter, enthusiasm*), but some on the third (e.g., *fundamental, correspondence*).

A number of commonly used multi-syllable words are usually pronounced without certain syllables (i.e., the ones in italics below are not pronounced in normal speech):

average, bus*i*ness, categ*o*ry, Cath*o*lic, comf*o*rtable, diff*e*rence, ev*e*ning, gen*e*ral, int*e*rested, int*e*resting, labor*a*tory, lit*e*rature, med*i*cine, pref*e*rable, ref*e*rence, temp*e*rature, veg*e*table, Wedn*e*sday

ACRONYMS

Acronyms are pronounced in three ways:

1. with each individual letter pronounced separately and with equal stress on each letter, for example, DVD, EU, UN, WWW
2. like a normal word, for example, NATO, UNESCO, URL
3. like a normal word but with vowel sounds added, for example, FTSE (pronounced *footsie*)

Chapter 11

Improve Your English with Audiovisual Resources

Factoids

❖ The inhabitants of countries which broadcast movies and other TV programs directly in English (e.g., Scandinavian countries, Holland, Portugal) tend to speak and understand English much better than those countries where movies are dubbed (France, Germany, Italy).

❖ In the 1930s and 1940s Germany, Italy and Spain dubbed British and US movies (i.e. replaced the English audio with that of their own language) to defend their national language and as a form of censorship to protect their regimes. It was also a problem of illiteracy as many people at that time would not have been able to read the subtitles. In Poland they initially used the same actor to dub every single part—male and female—of imported movies. The first countries to introduce subtitles were Denmark and France, in 1929.

❖ Dutch teenagers have a very wide vocabulary of everyday English because they tend to watch TV series—they thus hear the same expressions being said repeatedly over many episodes.

❖ The mayor of New York from 1933 to 1945 spoke English, Italian, and Yiddish fluently. If you watch his televised speeches with the volume off, you can still tell what language he was speaking in by noting his body language, particularly the way he used his hands and arms.

© Springer International Publishing Switzerland 2016
A. Wallwork, *English for Interacting on Campus*,
English for Academic Research, DOI 10.1007/978-3-319-28734-8_11

11.1 What's the buzz?

Answer the questions.

1. How can you improve your listening skills outside the classroom?
2. Which are easier to understand in English: movies or TV series? Why?
3. In your country are foreign TV shows and movies dubbed into your language? What are the pros and cons of watching them in the original language rather than the dubbed version?
4. Which are you favorite movies and TV series?
5. Are there some types of movies that are harder to understand than others (e.g. comedy vs science fiction)?
6. Do you ever watch documentaries in English? Why (not)?
7. When you watch in English, do you use subtitles? What are the pros and cons of using subtitles?
8. Apart from movies, TV series and music, what other resources can you find on YouTube to help you improve your English?
9. Do you watch TED presentations?
10. Do you watch the news in English? If so, which news service?

****

Many people rely on English lessons to improve their English without considering the fact that you can learn a considerable amount outside the classroom. Given that a major difficulty for most people is understanding native English speakers, it makes sense to take every opportunity you can to listen to English—in the car, on your phone, and on TV. This chapter gives advice on what to watch and how often.

In this chapter you will learn that:

- you need to be realistic when setting yourself listening tasks

- watching movies is more frustrating and less productive than watching most other types of TV programs

- how much you will understand will depend on the type of TV series you watch

- there are endless resources on the web to help you improve your listening skills

11.2   Set yourself a realistic objective

Be realistic about what you want to achieve. Just as you can't lose 10 kg in weight in one weekend, you can't learn English in two days.

Here are some ideas.

- watch the news in English once a day or one presentation on TED (see 11.4 below)

- watch two episodes of a 20-minute TV series or one episode of a 50-minute episode

But be patient. The first 10-20 times you watch you will only understand 10%. You should gradually manage to reach about 50%, and then hopefully even more.

Only watch things that you would have watched anyway in your own language. You are only going to learn if you are motivated and enjoy yourself.

Expose yourself to lots of different accents.

11.3   The news

Listening to the international news on TV or on the radio is good practice because you are probably already aware of some of the stories and you will thus be able to follow them much better. Watching news that is all local to one country is much more difficult.

Good stations to watch in Europe are: BBC News 24, BBC World News, Euronews, and RT.com.

In the US you can try: Fox, News Corp, Time Warner and CBS.

11.4 TED.com

This is a great website and in my opinion is probably the best way to improve your listening (apart, of course, from interacting directly with native speakers). The site is packed with fascinating talks (i.e., presentations) given by experts in various fields from around the world. You will learn not only English, but also interesting facts. You can

- choose the topic you are interested in by using their internal search engine—the main topics are technology, entertainment, design, business, science, culture, arts, and global issues

- choose the speaker

- choose the most watched talks, the most recent talks, the most talked about talks

- choose the length of the talk depending on the time you have available for watching—they vary from a minimum of around 2 minutes up to a maximum of around 20 minutes

- read a transcript of the talk either in English or in your own language—you can do this before you watch to get a clear idea of the topic, and also while you are watching. The transcript is interactive in the sense that you can click on words within the transcript and be automatically taken to that same point in the video

- use the subtitles—there are English subtitles for all the talks, and for the very popular talks there are often subtitles in many other languages

- download the talk and play it on other media

- read comments made by people who have watched the talk and contribute to a discussion on the topic

Note that the existence or not of subtitles and translations into various languages depends on how recently the talk was posted (if it is within the last few months, it may not have either of these features) and how popular the talk is.

If you are really serious about improving your listening, then another option is to copy and paste the transcript and invent your own listening exercises by deleting random words. Then listen a few days later (when you have forgotten the words!) and try to fill in the gaps.

For more details of how to use TED see Chapter 2 in the companion volume to this series entitled *English for Presentations at International Conferences*.

11.5   TV series

The main advantages of TV series are that they:

- can often be addictive, so you are really motivated to watch the next episode

- are shorter than movies (from 20 to 50 minutes maximum)—this makes finding time to watch them much easier

- show characters who keep reappearing so that you get tuned in to the voices; also these characters tend to have particular phrases that they say repeatedly

- go on for years, so you have a constant source of entertainment

11.6   Movies

Movies are much harder to understand because:

- the plot is totally new

- the voices are all new

- the film tends to last at least 90 minutes, which requires intense concentration

Nevertheless, watching movies is fun. So

- choose films you have already seen in your native language, so then you do not have to worry about following the plot

- check out on YouTube to hear what the actors sound like, and try to find extracts from the film to judge whether you are likely to enjoy it and understand it

- consider watching it over several days

For most non-native speakers, the easiest movies to understand tend to be

- science fiction—full of technical words that you may be familiar with, and there is little humor (humor tends to be quite difficult to understand)

- documentaries—the narrator tends to speak clearly and from a script, so even though you can't see the lips moving you will still be able to understand

- historical

The most difficult are ones that contain non-standard English, ones with lots of slang, and ones with a lot of humor and thus full of word plays, for instance:

- ones containing dialects

- wacky comedies

- thrillers

- crime stories

You might also consider watching old movies. Ones that precede the 1970s are often easier to understand as the actors tended to enunciate the words more clearly. Also, the plot is often slower and easier to follow.

11.7 Reality shows

If you want to hear "real" English, then watch a reality show. The problem is that reality shows contain a lot of slang which is (i) difficult to understand and (ii) unlikely to be very useful for you in the world of academia! However, such shows may help you to understand native English speaking students.

11.8 Dragon's Den

This TV program, which you can find on YouTube, was originally a Japanese 'reality show' in which contestants present their inventions, products and services in front of venture capitalists, who are real people with real money to invest).

There are four English language versions: British, Canadian, Irish and US (under the name Shark Attack). The Canadian version is fun and fast moving, but the British version is perhaps the easiest to understand, though rather serious. Dragon's Den makes great viewing because you will:

- learn useful business terminology and related phrases

- learn how to pitch (present in a very short period, one or two minutes) an idea

- see some incredibly good (and bad) inventions

Dragon's Den has the same advantage as a TV series (see 11.5), in that the main 'characters' – i.e. the venture capitalists – are the same throughout each series (though they sometimes change from series to series). This means that you will have a chance to get used to the dragons' voices and manner of speaking, thus you will tend to understand more and more, the more you watch.

11.9   YouTube

There are hundreds of thousands of short videos that you can watch on YouTube. The vast majority have no subtitles. However, many are simply fun. Let me just make one example. There are extracts from the shows of magicians and illusionists. These are great videos to watch because they are short and highly entertaining. You are also motivated to re-watch them to try and understand how the trick works. By watching them several times, you will also be hearing again and again what the magician says, and therefore hopefully improving your understanding.

11.10   Subtitles

There are no rules for the use of subtitles. The main problem is that if you use subtitles you will probably read the subtitles rather than listen. However, try to watch some parts of the video with subtitles and some without, or watch a part with subtitles and then re-watch the same part without subtitles.

If you do opt for subtitles, I suggest that you use English subtitles—select "English for the hard of hearing."

If there is a part that you simply don't understand, then switch on the subtitles from your language. It is also fun to watch films in your own language with English subtitles!

11.11   Songs

If you have any favorite English-speaking bands or singers, then try listening to their songs while reading the lyrics. They may contain a lot of slang but the ear-training that you will get will be very useful.

11.12   Audio books and podcasts

You can buy audio books and download podcasts on a huge variety of topics. If you put them on your iPod, you can then listen to them while you are traveling. The BBC provides a lot of downloadable materials (bbc.com).

Chapter 12

Automatic Translation: Pros and Cons

Factoids

❖ The European Commission (EC) was one of the pioneers of machine translation and at one time their translation service produced over one million pages per year. About one-third of the officials working in the European Union's (EU) institutions were once employed in connection with interpretation and translation. The cost of translation now accounts for around 1% of the EU budget. At the time of writing, the EU has 24 official and working languages. Originally all EU documents were translated into the language of the member countries; now due to time and money constraints, only a few have this privilege. According to the EC multilingualism website, the most multilingual EU citizens are those from Luxembourg, where 99% of people know at least one other foreign language, followed by Slovaks (97%) and Latvians (95%).

❖ Google Translate was introduced in 2007, initially with translations from French, German, and Spanish into English, and vice versa.

❖ Esperanto (meaning *one who hopes*) was a language devised by Dr Lazar Zamenhof, who was born in 1859 in Białystok, which at the time was in Russia but is now in Poland. Zamenhof felt that there could only be peace in the world if everyone spoke the same language so that no one would have a cultural advantage over anyone else. He published his work in 1887, during a period in which another 53 artificial universal languages were created. Esperanto has its own Wikipedia site—Vikipedio (eo.wikipedia.org), and Esperanto congresses are held every year. According to Wikipedia, the number of current speakers is estimated at between 250 and 5,000.

© Springer International Publishing Switzerland 2016
A. Wallwork, *English for Interacting on Campus*,
English for Academic Research, DOI 10.1007/978-3-319-28734-8_12

164

12.1 What's the buzz?

Imagine you wanted to translate the texts below into your own language.

In which cases do you think:

- a literal translation might work reasonably well?

- you could use the support of Google Translate or similar automated translation software?

- it would be better to translate manually, even if this would take a lot longer?

Text 1 student to prof

Dear Prof.,

Would you mind to sending us the slides of the second part of the lecture?

Thanks a lot in advance.

Text 2 student email to prof

Hi Mike,

Today was my last day of work placement. I didn't get a chance to say good-bye to you so I'm doing it now. Thank you for accommodating me in your lab, I really enjoyed my experience there.

Kind regards,

TEXT 3 STUDENT REPRESENTATIVE EMAIL TO FELLOW STUDENTS

Hello all

I have spoken to Prof Williams and this email is to report back to you on the aim of our session on Wednesday. Prof Williams informed me that the objective is to further define and translate our research questions into an appropriate empirical design.

As such, we have been asked to prepare 3-5 slides, situating and outlining a relevant (for our PhD) research question(s) and next proposing/arguing in favor of a relevant empirical research design (case studies, survey, databases,...) including the scale and scope of the empirical efforts that seem relevant.

We we will have a short presentation (5 slides maximum) followed by discussion/feedback.

The idea is to develop the backbone of one of the papers of our PhD.

TEXT 4 EXTRACT FROM STUDENT ASSIGNMENT

The results showed that tourists in front of important monuments who take selfies using selfie sticks and those who drop litter have an equivalent negative empathy value suggesting that such people should be considered under the category of 'majorly selfish'. Additional observations support our view: i) subjects of the selfie group had a mean lag time of 30.3 seconds between arriving at the monument and the onset of the need to take a photograph of themselves. ii) The mean time of the litter group between arrival and dropping cans and food packages was aligned with the expected response from the selfie group to being given a warning by the monument guards. iii) The MEMEME ego ratio in the selfie group was compatible with a destructive form of graffiti writing, and not significantly different from that found in the can't-see-the-writing-on-the-wall group. iv) No significant differences in the recurrence rate of Kudnt Givadam Syndrome (KGS) were observed between the groups.

*****

This chapter will help you how to assess whether or not to use automatic software to translate documents and emails. Throughout this chapter I will use the acronym GT to refer to Google Translate and automatic translation in general. Clearly, there are differences between for example, Bing and Google Translate, but for the purposes of this chapter such differences will be ignored. The penultimate section in this chapter refers to two wonderful online resources which you can use for translating words and phrases (and thus for checking your English): Reverso and Linguee.

12.2 The advantages of automatic translation

Automatic translation software, such as Bing and Google Translate (GT), is very useful for translating technical documents, and even emails providing they don't contain abbreviations and very informal expressions.

This accuracy strictly depends on

1. the language you are translating from - the greater the number of speakers of your language, the better the translation is likely to be
2. how much you modify the text of the original language before submitting it for translation

The second factor is crucial. Before submitting your text to GT, you need to make it more 'English' for example by:

- changing the word order to reflect English word order

- reducing the length of sentences

- replacing pronouns (e.g. *it, one, them*) with their respective nouns

- removing redundancy

Remember that GT does make mistakes, so you MUST revise the translation or get a native speaker to edit and proofread it for you.

12.3 Typical areas where Google Translate may make mistakes in English

If you decide to translate your manual using automatic software, you need to be aware of the kinds of mistakes the software might make. Below I have listed the most common mistakes which, at the time of writing, GT makes.

WORD ORDER

GT's main difficulty is with word order, i.e. the position of nouns, verbs, adjectives, and adverbs. If in your language you put the verb before its subject, or if you put an indirect object before the direct object, then GT will not be able to create the correct English order (i.e. the reverse of the order in your language).

PLURAL ACRONYMS

In English, we say *one CD* but *two CDs*. Most other languages do not have a plural form for acronyms, and thus say *two CD*.

GT is able to recognize this for common acronyms such as CD, DVD and PC, but not for very technical acronyms.

TENSES

GT sometimes changes the tense from the original. For example, you may use the future tense and GT will translate it into the present tense. In some cases, GT may be correct. For example, if in your language you say 'I will tell him when I *will see* him', GT will correctly translate this as 'I will tell him when I *see* him'. This is because in a time clause, *when* takes the present and not the future. However, very occasionally GT makes mistakes when it changes tenses, so it is wise to check very carefully.

UNCOUNTABLE NOUNS

An uncountable noun is a noun that cannot be made plural and which cannot be preceded by *a/an* or *one*. For example *information* is uncountable. This means you <u>cannot</u> say *an information, one information, two informations, several informations*.

The problem with uncountable nouns is that the surrounding words (i.e. articles, pronouns and verbs) must also be singular. This means that if, for example, *information* is countable in your language, GT will probably make errors with the surrounding words, as highlighted in this example (note: the example is NOT in correct English):

> *These* information *are* vital in order to understand xyz. In fact, *they are* so crucial that …

There are two solutions. You can modify your own language so that you put the surrounding words into the singular. Or you can check the English version. Whichever solution you use, the aim is to produce the following correct sentence:

> *This* information *is* vital in order to understand xyz. In fact, *it is* so crucial that …

or:

> *This* information *is* vital in order to understand xyz. In fact, *such information is* so crucial that …

VERY SPECIALIZED VOCABULARY

GT's dictionaries are huge but do not cover absolutely every word. If GT doesn't know a word, it will normally leave it in the original language.

WORDS WITH MORE THAN ONE MEANING

GT generally manages to guess the right meaning when translating into English because it looks at the surrounding words (i.e. how words are collocated together). In any case, you need to check carefully that GT has translated with the meaning you intended.

STRINGS OF WORDS USED IN COMPUTER TERMINOLOGY

If you use English phrases such as *status no-provider* in your own original language, sometimes GT will modify these when 'translating' and produce, for example, *provider-no status*. Essentially, you just need to check that any English in your source text has not been 'translated' by GT.

NAMES OF PEOPLE

At the time of writing, GT tends to translate people's first names and sometimes surnames. This should not be a problem in manuals as names of people do not usually appear. In any case, be aware that GT makes some rather unexpected translations.

ACCENTS AND SINGLE QUOTES

Does your native language use accents? If it does, then read on.

If you are, for example, French, then GT is helped considerably if you use the correct accents. Note how GT translates these two titles of a French medical paper in two ways depending on whether the accents are inserted or not. Interestingly, both translations would be possible, but one of the two might not reflect the author's real intention.

Mesurer la qualité de vie: une nécessité en thérapeutique cancérologique
GT: Measuring quality of life: a need *for therapeutic oncology*
Mesurer la qualite de vie: une necessite en therapeutique cancerologique
GT: Measuring quality of life: a need *in oncology therapeutics*

Below is the same paper title, but this time in Italian. In this case, if the accents are correctly inserted in the original text, then GT provides the correct translation. Unlike with French, GT also provides exactly the same translation if the accents are not inserted at all.

Misurare la qualità della vita: una necessità per l'oncologia terapeutiche

Misurare la qualita della vita: una necessita per l'oncologia terapeutiche

GT: Measuring the quality of life: a need for therapeutic oncology

But if the accent is placed after the final letter using a single quote (i.e. the ' character), which is a typical device used by those Italians who don't have accents on their keyboards, GT gets confused and thinks a quotation is being given.

Misurare la qualita' della vita: una necessita' per l'oncologia terapeutiche

GT: Measure the quality 'of life: a necessity' for Therapeutic Oncology

Of course, words may change meaning depending on whether there is an accent or not. Here are two examples in French:

Le poisson est sale = The fish is dirty.

Le poisson est salé = The fish is salty.

Les moines aiment les jeûnes = Monks like fasting.

Les moines aiment les jeunes = Monks like young people.

So if your language has accents, you need to be aware that GT may produce unusual results!

12.4   How to improve the chances of getting an accurate automatic translation

The success level of a Google translation depends to a large extent on how similar the construction of your language is with respect to the normal structure of English.

One solution is to modify the version in your own language before you submit it to translation. Some of the most important modifications to make are listed below.

To learn how to write well in English see Chapters 2 (word order), 3 (paragraphs), 4 (sentences), 5 (avoiding redundancy), 6 (avoiding ambiguity) in the companion volume *English for Writing Research Papers.*

SYNTAX

Put the subject as near as possible to the beginning of the sentence and the main verb next to it. Put adjectives before their associated nouns. Make sure that the direct object precedes the indirect object. For the rules of English word order.

DON'T SEPARATE THE SUBJECT FROM THE VERB

Limit the parts of your sentence to one or two. Here are some examples (the parts are divided by //)

> English is considered to be an easy language. [one part]
>
> English is the native language of around 400 million people, // and is often considered to be easy. [two parts]
>
> English, // the native language of around 400 million people, // is often considered to be easy. [three parts]

In the third sentence there are three parts, i) the subject (*English*), ii) a parenthetical phrase defining English (*the … people*), iii) the main part of the phrase (*is … easy*). GT is more likely to make mistakes if you write sentences where the subject (*English*) is split from its verb (*is*).

So keep your sentences simple.

Write one complete idea: *English is the native language of around 400 million people*

Then another complete idea: *and is often considered to be easy*

Do <u>not</u> write a series of partial bits of information. For example:

> English, the language spoken in England, which is part of the UK (which itself is made of four countries, i.e. England, Wales, Scotland and Northern Ireland), has a total number of native speakers - those whose English is their first language - of, according to current estimates, around 400 million people, making it the world's fourth most spoken languages in terms of native speakers after Mandarin Chinese, Hindi, and Spanish.

The shorter your sentences are, and the fewer the number of parts (i.e. phrases separated by punctuation), the better GT's translation will be.

PUNCTUATION

Different languages use punctuation in different ways. Before you submit your text for translation, if possible try to punctuate it in an English way. Keep the sentences short, replace semi colons with full stops, and where appropriate use commas to break up the various parts of the sentence.

USE ACTIVE RATHER THAN PASSIVE SENTENCES

The advantage of an active sentence is that it must contain a subject, and this subject must precede the verb (in English). This means that GT is likely to produce a more accurate translation.

REPLACE ANY PRONOUNS WITH THE NOUNS THAT THEY REFER TO

Pronouns in English can be very ambiguous because it may not be clear for the reader what they refer to. If you replace them with the noun they refer to, GT will make a more accurate translation. This is because Google works by looking for similar sequences of words in translations that it has already done. Words such as *it, they, them, one* can obviously be associated with many hundreds of thousands of other words. More concrete words such as *screen, mouse* and *modem* will be associated with fewer other words.

DO NOT USE SYNONYMS FOR KEY WORDS

The more synonyms you use to express the same concept , the greater the chance that GT will make a mistake. Imagine for example that you are a doctor. In this case, a key word would probably be *patient*. Consequently you should always use *patient*, rather than finding synonyms such as *subject, participant, member, case, sufferer* etc. In the field of medicine, the term *patient* is more specific than the other synonyms. GT may link the other synonyms with non medical cases, and thus choose the wrong translation.

12.5   Beware of the signs that Google Translate leaves behind

When checking a document that you have translated using Google Translate, in addition to checking for mistranslations, you should look out for:

- spaces that GT has inadvertently inserted before punctuation marks

- a small box-shaped symbol that may appear before certain words (this is a symbol that often appears when you cut and paste text from the web)

If you fail to do this, your professor will become immediately aware that i) you haven't checked your work, and ii) you translated it using automatic translation software.

Of course there is nothing ethically wrong in using GT. But in itself GT is not enough. Before submitting any automatically translated doc (or any doc, whether translated or not), you need to re-read it very carefully.

12.6   Do NOT use Google Translate to check your English

If you write something directly into English, you may think that you can use GT to check your English by translating it back into your own language to see if it makes sense. Unfortunately this does NOT work.

When you write in English you are naturally translating directly from your own language. So, if you submit your English text into GT and translate it back into your own language, the translated text in your own language will probably be very good because the structure of your English sentence is based on the structure of the same sentence in your language.

However, this does NOT indicate that your English version is correct. It only indicates that the resulting text in your own language is what you wanted to say in English.

For example, let's imagine you have written a non grammatical sentence such as *I am here since yesterday*. You have used the simple present (*I am*) because in your language this is the tense you would use. In reality in such cases the correct tense in English is the present perfect, so the sentence should be *I have been here since yesterday*.

If you get GT to translate *I am here since yesterday* into your own language, then GT's translation will probably look correct in your language because it is a literal translation. However, although the translation into your own language is correct, the original English is not correct (it should be: *I have been here*).

So, do not use GT to check the grammar of your English, instead see 12.8.

12.7 To see possible translations for a word or phrase in context use Reverso or Linguee

If you are not translating an entire document, but simply have a few words or phrases whose translation you are uncertain of, then you will find these two sites fantastic:

http://context.reverso.net/

http://www.linguee.com/

You can insert the phrase in your own language (the main European languages) and see how many other people have translated the same phrase into English. These two sites thus have massive advantages over Google Translate:

- translations are shown in context

- there are many examples of the same phrase translated into different ways - so you can choose the most appropriate

- they are real translations carried out by humans - obviously even humans can make mistakes, but there are so many examples given that you can be fairly sure that if 10 people have translated it all in the same way, then it's probably correct

So if you want to check your English, use Reverso or Linguee, but not GT.

12.8   Be careful of spelling

If words are misspelled in the original, then GT will either not translate them (if such a combination of letters does not exist – an English example would be *fomr*) or will mistranslate the word (e.g. *from* vs *form*).

GT uses US spelling. This is generally not a problem. But if your document requires UK spelling, then you will need to set your final spell check to UK spelling. Here are some examples:

US spelling: *behavior, catalog, center, color, modeled, modeling, program, signaling, traveled, traveling*

GB spelling: *behaviour, catalogue, centre, colour, modelled, modelling, programme, signalling, travelled, travelling*

Always use the spelling utility on your computer to check your spelling, although remember it won't check everything. Some of your misspellings will not be highlighted because they are words that really exist. When you have finished your document, do a 'find' and check if you have made any of the mistakes listed below. The first word in each case is probably the word you wanted to use:

addition vs addiction, assess vs asses, context vs contest, chose vs choice, drawn vs drown, thanks vs tanks, though vs tough, through vs trough, two vs tow, use vs sue, which vs witch, with vs whit

Other typical typos include:

form vs from, filed vs field, found vs founded, lose vs loose, relay vs rely, than vs then, three vs tree, weighed vs weighted

Chapter 13

Smileys, Acronyms, Txt Messg

❖ The smiley was first introduced to popular culture as part of a promotion by New York radio station WMCA beginning in 1962. Listeners who answered their phone "WMCA Good Guys!" were rewarded with a "WMCA good guys" sweatshirt that incorporated a happy face into its design (Wikipedia).

❖ To understand a Western smiley, you have to tilt your head: <> Amazed, %-) Confused and / or Drunk, :'-(Crying, :") Embarrassed, :-) Happy, (:-* Here's kissing you, :-D Laughing, :o Ooooh!!" shocked, :-(Sad, :-P Tongue in cheek, (:-(Very Unhappy, '-) Winking, l-O Yawning

❖ Japanese emoticons, *kaomoji*, are written horizontally and are consequently quicker and easier to understand:

  (^_^) or (^o^) Happy

  (>_<)> In trouble or a bit embarrassed

  (*^_^*) Embarrassed but happy

  m(_ _)m Apologetic

  (#^.^°) Shy

  (-_-#) Angry

  (@_@) Surprised

❖ In English slang, commonly used words are sometimes used with the opposite meaning, e.g. bad (=good), sick (=very good)

13.1 What's the buzz?

1. What do you think the following mean? Would any of them be used in a non-informal situation? Would any of them be appropriate to use with your professor?

    1. 2nite
    2. im2gud4u
    3. bbs
    4. fyi
    5. gf
    6. cya
    7. gonna
    8. wotcha
    9. footie
   10. def
   11. luv
   12. pls
   13. cuz
   14. :-ll
   15. :-(

****

This chapter is simply designed to be fun. It outlines many of the typical abbreviations used when writing very informal emails and text messages, and when chatting.

Note that such abbreviations, acronyms and phrases should NOT be used in a professional context.

Most of this chapter originally appeared in *Email and Commercial Correspondence*, which is part of the Springer series: *A Guide to Professional English*.

KEY 1) tonight, 2) I'm too good for you, 3) be back soon, 4) for your information [also commonly used in a more formal context], 5) girlfriend, 6) see you, 7) going to 8) what are you 9) football 10) definitely 11) love 12) please [also commonly used in a more formal context],13) because, 14) angry, 15) sad

13.2   Smileys

Smileys are also known as emoticons.

To see a very comprehensive list of Japanese emoticons: japaneseemoticons.net/

See also: https://en.wikipedia.org/wiki/List_of_emoticons

The table below shows how creative people have been in using the characters of the keyboard to create 'pictures'.

Amazed	:<>	Disgusted	:-|	Oh my god!	8-O
Angry	:-ll	Drinking every night	:*)	Sad	:-(
Big Hug	(((H)))	Drunk	:#)	Side splitting laughter	:-D
Big Kiss	:-X	Embarrassed	:")		
Can't believe it	:-C	Happy	:-)	Surprised/ shocked	:-O
Confused	:-S	Hungry	:0	Undecided	:-\
Crying	:'-(	Kiss	:-*	Winking	;-)
Cursing	:-@!	Laughing	:-D		
Disappointed	:-e	Makes no sense	:-S		

13.3   Numbers

Numbers occur quite frequently in the abbreviations used in chatlines, emails and text messages. Due to the bizarre spelling system of English, numbers can be used in many different ways:

   1) /won/, 2) /tu/, 3) /thri/ or /fri/, 4) /for/, 8) /eit/

The sound in 8 /eit/ can have many different spellings: *eight, ate, ait* (as in *wait*).

Below are some examples:

   1ce = *once*, every1 = *everyone*, hag1 = *have a good one* , ne1 = *anyone*, no1 = *no one*, som1 = *someone*, sum1 = *someone*, 2 = *to, too*, 2b = *to be* , 2day = *today*, 2moro = *tomorrow*, 2nite = *tonight*, f2f = *face to face*, f2t = *free to talk* , g2g = *got to go*, hrt2hrt = *heart to heart* , im2gud4u = *I'm too good for you*, se2e = *smiling ear to ear* , tlk2ul8r = *talk to you later*, wan2 = *want to*, wan2tlk = *want to talk?*, ru32nite = *are you free tonight?* , 4ever = *forever,* 4yeo = *for your eyes only* , b@thpics4 = *be at the pictures [cinema] for 8 pm* , b4 = *before,* b4n = *bye for now,* j4g = *just for grins,* plz 4gv me = *please forgive me,* bhl8 = *be home late,* cub l8r = *call you back later,* cul8er = *see you later,* d8 = *date* , gr8 = *great,* h8 = *hate,* l8 = *late,* l8er = *later,* m8 = *mate,* rungl8 = *running late,* w8 = *wait* , w84m = *wait for me,* w8in4u = *waiting for you*

13.4 Acronyms

A quick way of writing is to use acronyms, where each letter stands for a word. Below are some examples:

a/s/l? = *age/sex/location?,* afaict = *as far as I can tell* , afaik = *as far as I know* , afair = *as far as I remember* , afk = *away from keyboard* , aka = *also known as,* asap = *as soon as possible,* atb = *all the best,* ayor = *at your own risk,* bak = *back at the keyboard,* bbl = *be back late(r),* bbn = *bye bye now,* bbs = *be back soon,* bf = *boy friend,* bfn = *bye for now,* btdt = *been there done that,* btw = *by the way,* cm = *call me* , crb = *come right back,* dqmot = *don't quote me on this,* dtrt = *do the right thing,* dwb = *don't write back,* dwisnwid = *do what I say not what I do* , eiok = *everything is OK* , emfbi = *excuse me for butting in,* eom = *end of message,* fc = *fingers crossed,* fwiw = *for what it's worth,* fya = *for your amusement* , fye = *for your entertainment* , fyi = *for your information,* ga = *go ahead* , gal = *get a life,* gf = *girl friend* , gl = *good luck,* gmab = *give me a break,* gmta = *great minds think alike,* gw = *good work* , h&k = *hug and kiss,* hagn = *have a good night,* hand = *have a nice day,* ht = *hi there,* hth = *hope this helps,* hwru = *how are you?* , hyt = *hey you there* , idk = *I don't know* , imho = *in my humble opinion,* ims = *I am sorry,* iow = *in other words,* iyswim = *if you see what I mean,* jam = *just a minute* , jic = *just in case,* jk = *just kidding,* kit = *keep in touch,* lol = *laughing out loud,* ltm = *laugh to myself,* myob = *mind your own business,* nw = *no way,* obtw = *oh, by the way* , omg = *oh, my god* , sohf = *sense of humor failure* , sol = *smiling out loud,* ta = *thanks again,* tafn = *that's all for now,* tgif = *thank god it's Friday,* tia = *thanks in advance,* toy = *thinking of you,* tptb = *the powers that be,* ttbomk = *to the best of my knowledge* , ttyl = *talk to you later,* tu = *thank you,* uw = *you're welcome,* wayd = *what are you doing?,* wb = *welcome back,* wrt = *with regard to / with respect to,* wu = *what's up?,* wud? = *what you doing?,* wuf? = *where are you from?,* wysiwyg = *what you see is what you get*

13.5   How sounds of letters are used

Letters have always been used in English instead of words. The most commonly used until the advent of the internet was probably IOU which stands for *I owe you* to indicate that you owe someone money, for example *IOU $10* means *I owe you ten dollars.* Below are some examples:

b = *be,* bcnu = *be seeing you,* c = *see,* cya = *see ya,* how ru = *how are you,* ic = *I see,* ilq = *I like you* , oic = *oh, I see,* qt = *cutie,* r u there? = *are you there?* , r = *are,* ru cmng = *are you coming?,* ru = *are you?,* ruok = *are you ok?,* sup = *what's up?,* thanq = *thank you,* tq = *thank you,* u = *you,* uok = *you ok?,* ur = *you are,* wru = *where are you?* , y = *why*

13.6   Use of symbols

In the examples below & stands for *and,* and @ for *at,* even in the middle of words.

l&n	*landing*		ura*	*you are a star*
pl&	*planned*		x	*kiss*
po$bl	*possible*		xoxox	*hugs and kisses*
s^	*what's up?*		cu@	*see you at*
th@	*that*			

13.7 Contractions

The words below have been around for decades as part of the spoken language and also in rock, rap and blues lyrics. They are contractions of two or more words, which imitate the sound of English spoken quickly. In the table below, the first column is the contraction, the second the full form, and the third an example.

ain't	*has not, am not*	You ain't seen nothing yet.
betchu	*I bet you*	I betchu $100 that I am right.
betta	*I had better*	Betta go now.
coulda	*could have*	Coulda told you that myself.
cuppa	*a cup of (tea)*	Gonna have a cuppa.
dunno	*I don't know*	How much does it cost? Dunno.
gimme	*give me*	Gimme your email.
gonna	*I am going to*	Gonna tell all my friends.
gotta ...?	*have you got ..?*	Gotta minute?
gotta	*I have got to*	Gotta go now.
hiya	*hi there*	Hiya, how are you doing?
izzy	*is he*	Izzy someone special for you?
kinda	*kind of*	I kinda like it.
lemme	*let me*	Lemme get this clear.
lotta	*a lot of*	A whole lotta love.
mighta	*might have*	Mighta told me u were married.
outta	*out of*	Gotta get outta here.
shaddup / shadap	*shut up*	Shaddup will you?
shoulda	*should have*	Shoulda seen his face when I told him.
sorta	*sort of*	It's sorta like a dream.
soundsa	*it sounds like a*	Soundsa a good idea.
sup, wazzup	*what's up*	Sup mate?
wanna	*want to*	Wanna go out tonight?
watcha, wotcha	*what are you, what do you*	Wotcha gonna do about it?
wouldna	*would not*	I wouldna wanna do that again.

13.8 Short forms

For centuries English has been a language which has liked to simplify itself by reducing the length of long words. Some have been with us for so long that we no longer even notice that orginally they were much longer, for example, *fax – facsimile*. Here are some examples:

ad = *advertisement*, add = *address*, brill = *brilliant*, coll = *college*, comp = *computer*, convo = *conversation*, cred = *credit (on mobile phone), credibility*, def = *definitely*, fav = *favorite*, info = *information*, min = *minute*, mob = *mobile*, mos def = *most definitely*, pic, pik = *picture, photo*, prob = *problem*, sec = *second*, tel = *telephone*, typo = *typography mistake*, uni = *university*

13.9 Abbreviations

An abbreviation just uses some letters (generally just the consonants) of the original word. It thus differs from a short form (13.8) which only uses the initial letters (both consonants and vowels) of a word. Here are some examples:

b'day = *birthday*, bk = *break*, cfm = *confirm* , ctr = *center*, dnr = *dinner* , frm = *from*, grt = *great*, lsr = *loser*, lv = *love*, msg = *message*, n = *and*, nxt = *next*, pls / plz = *please*, ppl = *people*, rgds = *regards*, smt / smthg = *something*, spk = *speak*, thx, tnx, tx = *thanks*, txt = *text* , w/o = *without*, wknd = *weekend*, wrk = *work* , yr = *your*

13.10 Alternative spellings

Text messaging and chatlines have had a huge impact on the way English words are now being spelt in informal contexts. The spellings tend to be much more phonetical, i.e. to reflect more closely the way the words are pronounced:

flirtz, ladz, loadz	flirts, lads, loads ($z = s$ plural and s third person singular)
gettin, interestin	getting, interesting (final g cut)

Sometimes the way a word is spelt will reflect the part of the English-speaking country where someone is from:

wid	with
wit	with
wiv	with

Below are some more examples:

afta = *after,* alrite = *alright,* ansa = *answer,* av = *have,* 'avin' = *having,* bin = *been,* bk = *back,* bout = *about,* coz, cuz = *because,* d, da or de = *the,* dem = *them,* dere = *there,* doin = *doing,* dun = *done,* eva = *ever,* ez = *easy,* fankz = *thanks,* fella = *fellow,* footie = *football,* gd = *good,* gudluk = *good luck,* hun = *honey,* iv = *I've,* jus = *just,* kann = *can,* keul, kool = *cool,* laf = *laugh,* lata = *later,* lurve = *love,* luv = *love,* mite = *might,* n = *and,* nah = *no,* ne = *any,* nething = *anything,* no = *know,* nufn = *nothing* , 'ome = *home,* ov = *of,* prolly = *probably,* recked = *wrecked,* rite = *right,* sed = *said,* shud = *should,* skool = *school,* soz = *sorry,* spose = *suppose,* ter = *to,* tho = *though,* uz = *us,* wel = *well,* wen = *when,* wi = *with,* wid = *with,* wit = *with,* wiv = *with,* wot = *what,* wud = *would,* wudnt = *wouldn't,* wus, wuz = *was,* xlnt = *excellent,* yas = *you,* yer = *yes*

Chapter 14

Useful Phrases

What the experts say

Many writers perplex their readers and hearers with mere nonsense. Their writings need sunshine. Pure and neat language I love, yet plain and customary.

Ben Jonson (1572–1637) English Renaissance dramatist, poet and actor,
and contemporary of William Shakespeare

The Latin tongue, long the vehicle used in distributing knowledge among the different nations in Europe, is daily more and more neglected; and one of the modern tongues, viz. French, seems, in point of universality, to have supplied its place. It is spoken in all the courts of Europe; and most of the literati, those even who do not speak it, have acquired knowledge of it, to enable them easily to read the books that are written in it. This gives a considerable advantage to that nation. It enables its authors to inculcate and spread through other nations, such sentiments and opinions, on important points, as are most conducive to its interests, or which may contribute to its reputation, by promoting the common interests of mankind.

Benjamin Franklin (1706–1790) American author,
scientist, inventor, statesman, and diplomat

Every language … has its own inseparable and incommunicable qualities of superiority.

Thomas de Quincey (1785–1859),
English author and intellectual

The sum of human wisdom is not contained in any one language, and no single language is capable of expressing all forms and degrees of human comprehension.

Ezra Pound (1885–1972),
American expatriate poet and critic

© Springer International Publishing Switzerland 2016
A. Wallwork, *English for Interacting on Campus*,
English for Academic Research, DOI 10.1007/978-3-319-28734-8_14

14.1 What's the buzz?

Discuss the questions.

1. Research conducted on the Michigan Corpus of Academic Spoken English revealed that saying *I think* is around 250 times more common than saying *in my opinion*. Does this mean that there is no point in learning phrases that are used so infrequently?

2. Is it important to learn both the informal and formal versions of particular phrases? Why?

3. How can learning useful phrases help you improve your listening?

4. Is it always a good idea to understand the grammar of a particular phrase or to understand the exact meaning of the individual words in a phrase? For example *I look forward to seeing you.*

5. Is it important to learn (and use) slang expressions?

****

This chapter is designed to provide you with useful phrases for many of the verbal and email interactions you will have on campus with academic staff and fellow students. Most of the phrases are either neutral or slightly formal - this means that you can use them with practically everyone.

This chapter does <u>not</u> cover slang expressions or phrases that would be appropriate for leisure activities (e.g. sports, parties, concerts). The main focus is on phrases for expressing opinions and (dis)agreement, clarifying and explaining, participating in class, communicating with professors, socializing, and other related activities.

You will see that there are a lot of phrases! You don't need to learn them all or use them all. However, it will help you considerably if you familiarize yourself with them so that at least you will hear and recognize them when they are used by others.

This chapter also includes phrases for topics that are not covered in the book itself, i.e. going to bars and cafes, and traveling and hotels.

This chapter does NOT include phrases for writing emails. These can be found in Chapter 14 of the companion volume: *English for Academic Correspondence.*

14.2   Asking for and giving help

Asking for and giving directions on campus

Excuse me, do you know where xx building is?

Can you tell me where the course is taking place?

Do you know where Professor Smith's room is?

I'm looking for the computer lab. Do you know where it is?

It's next to the canteen.

It's upstairs on the third floor. Go up those stairs over there. Get to the third floor and turn right. Go down to the end of the corridor and there is a glass door. Go through the door and her office is the first door on the right.

Go out of the building. Make a left / Turn left. You should be able to see a tall building at the end of the road. Well the building you're looking for is just to the right of the tall building.

Go up Green Street, left at the traffic lights, then second right.

Offering directions

Can I help you?

You look lost, do you need any help?

Enquiring

I wonder if you could help me?

Do you know where/how I could … ?

Do you happen to know if … ?

Excuse me, do you think you could … ?

Responding to an enquiry

Yes, of course.

Certainly. Sure. Yes, what's the problem?

No, I'm sorry I don't actually.

I don't actually, but if you ask that man …

Actually, I can't I'm afraid.

Requesting help

Do you think could you give me a hand with …?

Would you mind helping me with …?

I wonder if you could help me with …?

Could you give me some help?

Could you do me a favor?

Would you like me to give you a hand with …?

Accepting request for help

Sure. No problem.

Two seconds and I'll be with you.

OK. Right. Where shall I start?

Declining request for help

I'm sorry but I can't just at the moment.

Sorry, but you've caught me at a bad time.

Offering help

Shall I help you with …?

Do you want me to help you with …?

If you want, I could give you hand with that.

Are you sure you don't need any help with that?

Accepting offer of help

That's really kind of you.

Great thanks.

If you're sure you can spare the time, that'd be great.

If you really don't mind, that'd be most helpful.

Declining offer of help

That's very kind of you but I think I can manage.

No, it's alright thanks.

Thanks but I really don't want to put you out.

Generic apologies and responses

I'm really sorry.

Oh that's alright.

Don't worry.

Not to worry.

I'm sorry about that.

These things happen.

No problem.

I'm sorry about that. I'll get on to it straight away.

Brilliant, that would be great, thank you.

Apologizing for misunderstandings

Sorry, I didn't mean to …

Sorry, I thought you meant …

I meant …

I didn't mean to offend.

Sorry I obviously didn't make myself clear.

Thanking

Thank you / Thanks very much.
You've been most / really helpful.
Thank you very much for your help.
Sorry to have troubled you.

Brilliant. Cheers.
Not at all.
You're welcome.
Don't mention it.

14.3 Asking about courses, services, associations

Courses

Excuse me, can you tell me what documents I will need to register for the courses?

Which courses are compulsory? Which courses am I required to enroll on?

How many credits are there for the course on …?

Are there any online courses that I should consider?

Student support services

Where is the student support office?

How do I get a doctor?

What documents do I need to get a bank account?

Am I insured to do laboratory work?

Is there any accommodation that I could have on campus while I look for a flat in the town?

I am not sure how to complete this rental application form. Can you help me?

Where is the local mosque?

Is there free Internet?

How do I get a travel card?

Can you recommend where I can buy a second hand bicycle and a lock?

Student associations

I am interested in rock-climbing. Are there any clubs I can join?

I would like to get involved with decisions regarding university policies. Is this possible?

Are there any political groups on campus?

Is it possible to learn a martial art?

What are fraternities and sororities?

14.4 Questions to ask your tutor / professor when you first meet

Addressing each other

First of all, how should I address you?

Thanking

Thank you very much for agreeing to be my supervisor, I really appreciate it.

Discussing how your relationship will work

I have a series of questions about how our relationship is going to work. Is it OK if I ask you them now?

Can I ask you what is your primary goal in supervising me?

You have read my research proposal, do you think my goals match your goals?

Realistically, how much will you be able to help me in carrying out my research?

Do you plan to use my research for other purposes?

I notice that you are not an expert in my exact field, do you think this might cause any problems or actually be a benefit?

Deciding on when to meet and means of communication

How often will we meet and where? Can I just drop by your office, or will everything be pre-scheduled? I actually work well to a routine if that's OK with you.

Is it OK if I email you reasonably frequently?

Will you be expecting me to do some teaching?

14.5 Making arrangements for meetings with your professor

Introducing topic of meeting face to face

Professor, could I just have a word with you?

Professor, could I ask you a favor?

Explaining your reasons for wanting the meeting

The thing is I don't think I will be able to meet the deadline.

I'm having some problems understanding …

Suggesting the time

Let's arrange a call so that we can discuss it further.

Would it be possible for us to meet on …?

Could we meet some time next week?

When would be a good time?

What about December 13?

Would Friday at 4 o'clock suit you?

Would tomorrow morning at 9.00 suit you?

Can we arrange a Skype call for 15.00 on Monday 21 October?

Responding positively

OK, that sounds like a good idea.

Yes, that's fine.

Yes, that'll be fine.

That's no problem.

Informing of unavailability at that time

No, sorry. I can't make it then.

I'm afraid I can't come on that day.
Sorry but I can't make it that day.

Showing empathy with a busy professor

It's really only a couple of slides that I need you to look at.

I don't think it will take more than five minutes of your time.

I realise that you may not have time. So if you can't, no problem.

I realise that this is all very last minute, so I will understand if you can't …

If you don't have time, then no problem.

Changing the time

Unfortunately, I'll have to cancel our meeting on …

I'll be unable to make the meeting.

We were due to meet next Tuesday afternoon. Is there any chance I could move it until later in the week? Weds or Thurs perhaps?

Could we fix an alternative?

Can we fix a new time? How about …?

Arriving at the meeting

Good morning, I am Haana, the student from Iran. You may remember we met briefly last week.

May I come in?

Do you have a minute?

Is this a good time?

The reason I have come to see you is:

I was wondering whether you could …

Would you have five minutes to explain …?

Terminating the meeting

Well, thank you very much. You've been really helpful.

Would it be OK if I came back at the same time next week?

Thanks again, and see you at this afternoon's workshop.

Sorry to interrupt you Professor Smith, but I've got a class in ten minutes. Would it be OK to continue the discussion next week?

Yes, I think I've understood what you are saying. Unfortunately I need to go now because there's a workshop I need to attend.

14.6 Clarifying what your professor has just said (in class)

Introducing what you are going to say

I just wanted to say ..

Sorry, I was just going to say that …

Indicating you haven't understood a specific concept

I'm not really sure how it works.

I don't see why …

How come that wouldn't …?

But that's not efficient, is it?

But how can we …?

Indicating you've lost the complete thread (i.e. the complete logic of the professor's argument or explanation)

Sorry, but I'm lost.

Sorry, but you've lost me.

I don't know about the others, but I can't follow what you are saying.

Asking a fellow student if he/she has understood

What did she just say?

Are you following what he's saying?

What did she mean when she said …?

What does x mean in this context?

Do you think we should ask him to slow down?

Checking on what exercises and readings have been assigned

Sorry, but I am not sure which book you are referring to.

So when exactly is the exam, sorry?

So what will the test cover?

When is the assignment due?

Is there any flexibility in that deadline?

14.7 Understanding native speakers and clarifying

Asking the speaker to change their way of speaking

Sorry, could you speak up please?

Sorry, could you speak more slowly please?

Asking for repetition of the whole phrase

I'm sorry what did you say?

Could you explain that again using different words?

Sorry, could you say that again?

Sorry, I didn't catch that.

Sorry what was your question?

Identifying the part of the phrase that you did not understand

Sorry, what did you say at the beginning?

I didn't get the middle bit / last bit.

Sorry what was the last bit?

Could you say that last bit again?

Sorry I missed the bit about …

And you did "what" sorry?

And you went "where" sorry?

You spoke to "who" sorry?

Repeating the part of the phrase up to the point where you stopped understanding

Sorry, you thought the presentation was … ?

And then you went to … ?

And the food was …?

When the speaker has repeated what they said but you still cannot understand

Sorry, I still don't understand.

Sorry, do you think you could say that in another way?

Sorry, could you say that again but much more slowly?

Sorry, could you write that word down, I can't really understand it.

When you understand the words but not the general sense

Sorry, I'm not really clear what you're saying.

Sorry I think I am missing / have missed the point.

Sorry but I am not really clear about …

When you didn't hear because you were distracted

Sorry, I missed that last part.

Sorry, I got distracted. What were you saying?

Sorry, I've lost track of what you were saying.

Sorry, I've forgotten the first point you made.

Sorry, I'm a bit lost.

Sorry I wasn't concentrating, what were you saying?

Clarifying by summarizing what other person has said

So what you're saying is …

So you're saying that it is true.

So if I understood you correctly, you mean …

Let me see if I have the big picture. You're saying that …

Clarifying what you have said

What I said / meant was …

What I'm trying to say is …

The point I'm making is …

Let me say that in another way.

In other words, what I mean is …

Clarifying a misunderstanding in what you said

No, that's not really what I meant.

No, actually what I meant was …

Well, not exactly.

What I was trying to say was …

That's not actually what I was trying to say.

Clarifying a misunderstanding in what someone else said

I think you may have misunderstood what he said. What he meant was …

No, I think what he was trying to say was … Have I got that right?

If I'm not mistaken, what she was saying was …

Checking that others are following you

Does that make sense to you?

Do you understand what I mean?

Do you understand what I'm saying?

Saying that you are or are not following someone else

Yes, I see what you're getting at.

Yes, perfectly.

Yes, I know what you are saying …

Yeah, yeah, yeah—I've got you.

I'm with you.

OK, I think it's clear what you are saying.

Well, no not really, could you explain it again?

When you get lost while you are speaking

Sorry, I've forgotten what I was going to say.

Sorry, I've lost track of what I was saying.

Sorry, I can see I'm not making much sense.

Sorry, I don't really know what I am talking about.

14.8 Giving opinions and making suggestions

Giving opinions

I think/reckon we should …

What I think is …

I honestly think that …

The way I see it …

It seems to me that …

Agreeing

I agree

Right.

You're right there.

I think you're right.

Yes, definitely.

Exactly!

Precisely!

I couldn't agree more.

Giving signs that you are rejecting a suggestion

Yes, but …

OK, but …

I get what you're saying but …

Diplomatic disagreement

I see what you mean, but …

You've got a point, but …

I take/see your point but …

I appreciate what he's saying but …

I appreciate your point of view but …

You may be right, but personally I …

I'm not sure whether that's feasible.

I don't want to sound discouraging but …

I can see why you want to do this but …

OK, but what if …?

Yes, but have you thought about …?

Making suggestions
What about …?

Why don't we …?

What I think we should do is …

We should/ought to …

If I were you I would …

Maybe you should / could …

You might want to …

Could you maybe …

Making tentative suggestions
We could always …

It might be a good idea to …

Have you thought of …?

One solution would be to …

What about …?

I wonder if we could …

14.9 Interrupting and dealing with interruptions in study groups, seminars and workshops

Interrupting your interlocutor
Excuse me for interrupting.

I'd like to comment on that.

If I could just interrupt you …

OK, but listen …

Sorry, could I just interrupt?

Sorry do you mind if I just say something?

What to say when someone interrupts you
Sorry, just a sec …

OK, I've nearly finished …

Sorry, if I could just finish what I'm saying …

Can I just finish what I was saying? It will only take me a minute.

Sorry, just one more thing, …

Sorry, can I just say / add something.

I would just like to add that …

Returning to what you were just saying before an interruption
As I was saying …

Going back to what I was saying / I said before …

Let's just go back a bit to what we were saying before.

Can I just go back …

Let's get back to the point.

I think we're losing sight of the main point. .

Returning to main point after an interruption (e.g. a phone call)
OK, where was I? / What was I going to say?

OK, what we were saying? Oh, yes, I was saying that …

Asking the main speaker to go back to a previous point
Could we just back to what you were saying about …

Would you mind going over what you were saying about …

Before the break you were saying that …

Can I ask something about what you were saying earlier?

Beginning a parenthesis
By the way, did you know that Silvia is …

By the way, I forgot to tell you that …

On a completely different subject …

If I could just change the subject a second …

Pausing for time
I mean. Well. Right. Um. Er. You know.

Could we come back to that later?

Now where was I?

Sorry, I'll just have to think about that a sec.

Sorry, I've forgotten what I was going to say.

14.10   Invitations

Suggesting going to the bar / cafe
Shall we go and have a coffee?

Would you like to go and get a coffee?

What about a coffee?

Do you have a coffee machine in the company?

No we usually go to a bar - it's only a few meters away.

Offering drink / food at the bar / cafe
Can I get you anything?

No, nothing for me thanks.

What can I get you?

I'll have a coffee please.

Would you like a coffee?

I think I'll have an orange juice.

Black or white? How many sugars?

So, what would you like to drink?

Would you like some more tea?

Shall I pour it for you?

When you need to leave the bar / cafe
Is there a bathroom here?

Well, I think we'd better get back - the next meeting starts again in ten minutes.

Shall we get back?

Formal invitations for dinner
Would you like to have lunch next Friday?

If you are not busy tonight, would you like to …?

We're organizing a dinner tonight, I was wondering whether you might like to come?

I'd like to invite you to dinner.

Accepting
That's very kind of you. I'd love to come. What time are you meeting?

Thank you, I'd love to.

That sounds great.

Responding to an acceptance
Great. OK, well we could meet downstairs in the lobby.

Great. I could pass by your hotel at 7.30 if you like.

Declining
I'm afraid I can't, I'm busy on Friday.

That's very nice of you, but …

No, I'm sorry I'm afraid I can't make it.

Unfortunately, I'm already doing something tomorrow night.

Responding to a non-acceptance
Oh that's a shame, but not to worry.

Oh well, maybe another time.

14.11   Socializing

Introducing yourself
Hi.

Hi, I'm Riccardo.

By the way, I'm Kalinda.

By the way, my name is Kalinda Abbas.

Sorry, I have not introduced myself - I'm Kalinda Abbas from Pakistan.

Pleased to meet you. I'm Zahra Rahman. I'm from Iran.

When you didn't catch their name
Sorry, I didn't catch your name.

Sorry, I didn't get your name clearly. Can you spell it for me?

Sorry, how do your pronounce your name?

Commenting on assignments / tests / exams
I thought the test was incredibly / ridiculously hard.

The exam wasn't too bad, was it?

I found the first part really difficult.

How did they expect us to read so much?

There's no way I am going to be able to complete the assignment on time.

Finding out where someone comes from
So where are you from exactly?

So are you from NY?

No, I'm from Poland

Ah from Poland?

Oh really, so what brought you to NY?

So how do you find NY?

Whereabouts is *place*? Where exactly is *place*?
How big is it?

I've heard there is a famous building in *place*,
but I can't remember the name?

Is it true that it's famous for windsurfing? How come?

What is the weather like there?

Holidays

Have you taken any holiday yet this year?

Where did you go last year?

Had you been there before?

Guest questions to host

Do you live anywhere near here?

How long does it take you to get to work?

Do you come by car?

Family

So, do you have any brothers and sisters?

And you parents, what do they do?

Talking about language skills

How and where did you learn English?

Does your husband / wife speak English?

How many languages do you speak fluently?

Do you speak any other languages?
How difficult is your language to learn for a
foreigner?

For me it's quite difficult to express emotions
or complex ideas in another language, do you
find this too?

Discussing differences between countries

*The examples below refer to questions that an
Italian asks a Spaniard with regard to differences between Italy and Spain. However, the
questions could be adapted so as to refer to any
country.*

What do you think are the main differences
between Italy and Spain?

Do you find the Italians are similar to the
Spanish?

How similar do you think Italy and Spain are?

What are the differences between our life style
and yours?

What are the main differences between the
Spanish and Italian way of life?

Are there many differences between the way
Spanish men and Italian men behave?

What do the Spanish think about the Italians?

I am going to be moving to Spain quite soon –
do you think it's a nice place to live?

Talking about food

What do you think of the food here? How does
it compare with food in your country?

Have you tried any of the local dishes?

Do you have any particular national / local
dishes in your country?

What do you normally have for lunch in your
country?

What do you miss about food from your own
country?

Have you been to any restaurants here? How do
the prices compare with restaurants in your
country?

Have you tried the wine here?

Do people drink alcohol in your country?

Discussing politics

*Politics can be a very dangerous topic, so be
very careful when asking the questions below.*

I'm curious to know if people in your country
approve of your [left / right-wing]
government?

What is the situation with x at the moment?

What does the general public / do the people
think about x?

I have heard that your government has banned
x – what reaction did this have? How has this
impacted on life in your country?

What is the attitude to …?

Do you know anything about politics in my
country?

What do you think about our politicians? And
our current government?

What does the press in your country say about
our …?

What do you think about our public services
(schools, national health system, transport)?

Someone who has moved to your country

*Note: The following phrases are related to
questions to someone who is living in Vietnam
but is not native to Vietnam. Obviously you
could substitute Vietnam / Vietnamese for whatever country you wish to talk about.*

Why did you decide to move to Vietnam?

How long have you been living here?

Had you ever been to Vietnam before?

Where did you live before coming to Vietnam?

How are you managing here in Vietnam? Are you learning much Vietnamese?

What have you seen in Vietnam?

Where have you been in Vietnam?

What do you think about Vietnam? And the life here?

What in particular do you like about Vietnam?

What do you think of the Vietnamese?

Have you made friends easily?

Are you going to stay here for a long time?

Do you have any particular plans for the future?

Are you planning on staying here or where else would you like to live?

What do you miss most about your home country?

Showing interest
Oh, are you?

Oh, is it?

Oh, really?

Right.

That's interesting.

Oh, I hadn't realized.

Giving advice
Have you thought about … ?

Don't you think perhaps you should … ?

Perhaps it might not be a bad idea to …

If I were you I'd …

Maybe the best thing would be to …

Perhaps you ought to/should …

Showing enthusiasm
That's wonderful/great/fantastic/perfect.

Well done! Congratulations! Good on you.

That's marvelous news. I'm so pleased for you.

Really? I can hardly believe it.

You must be so proud of yourself.

14.12   Leaving and saying goodbye

Making excuses for leaving
I am sorry – do you know where the bathroom is?

It was nice meeting you but sorry I just need to go to the bathroom (GB) / restroom (US).

Sorry but I just need to answer this call / I have just remembered I need to make an urgent call.

It has been great talking to you, but I just need to make a phone call.

Sorry, I've just seen someone I know.

Sorry, but someone is waiting for me.

Listen, it has been very interesting talking to you but unfortunately I have to go … maybe we could catch up with each other tomorrow.

Using the time as an excuse for leaving
Does anyone have the correct time because I think I need to be going?

Oh, is that the time? I'm sorry but I have to go now.

Sorry, I've got to go now.

I think it's time I made a move.

Wishing well and saying goodbye
Informal

It's been very nice talking to you.

I hope to see you again soon.

I really must be getting back.

I do hope you have a good trip.

It was a pleasure to meet you.

Please send my regards to Dr Hallamabas.

Informal

Be seeing you.

Bye for now.

Keep in touch.

Look after yourself.

Say 'hello' to Kate for me.

See you soon.

See you later.

Take care.

See you in March at the conference then.

Hope to see you before too long.

Have a safe trip home.

OK, my taxi's here.

Nice to have met you.

Give my regards to Julia.

Say hello to Stefan.

Have a nice time!

Thanks very much, the same to you.

14.13   Traveling and hotels

Buying air tickets
Is there a flight to …?

When does it leave / take off?

When does it arrive / land?

What time do I have to check in?

I'd like to book a return / round-trip flight to …

I'd like to cancel / change my reservation on flight number …

Buying train tickets
What's the fare to …?

Do I have to change?

When does it arrive at …?

Which platform does the train leave from / arrive at?

I'd like a single / one-way ticket to …

How much is a return / round-trip to *place* in first class?

I'd like to reserve a seat.

Dealing with taxis
Could you get me a taxi?

Where is the taxi rank / stand?

To the station please.

Please stop here.

Could you wait for me?

I'll be back in 10 minutes.

How much do I owe you?

Keep the change.

Giving directions
Go straight ahead.

It's on the left/right.

Opposite / behind …

Next to / After …

Turn left at the … next corner / traffic lights.

Take the A3.

You have to go back to …

Reserving a hotel room
Your hotel has been recommended to me by …

Please could you reserve me a single / double) room from …

How much is it per night, half board / full board, please?

Do you take credit cards?

Is breakfast included?

I'd like a single room for two nights.

I'd like a room with a shower.

I'll be arriving late.

How much does it cost?

Do you accept credit cards?

We would like to change our reservation at your hotel from *date* to *date*.

I would be grateful if you would confirm this booking.

Asking about hotel location and facilities
Could you please send us information about the hotel, its locations and the facilities you offer, plus details of your rates.

Could you please let us know where your hotel is located with respect to the centre of the town.

Could you send me a list of the agencies organizing guided tours in your region?

I'd like to know if you organize trips to *place*.

Do you organize any trips where it is possible to practice *sport*?

Arriving at hotel

My name's …

I've got a reservation for two nights.

I have a reservation in the name of …

The booking was confirmed both by email and fax.

Which floor is my room on?

When will it be ready?

Has anyone else from my company arrived here already?

I will be leaving at 08.30 tomorrow morning.

Asking about services

Is there an Internet connection?

Is there a shuttle bus to *place*?

Can you book me a taxi?

Is there a train that goes to the *place*?

What time do I have to be back at the hotel?

When is breakfast served?

I'm expecting Mr X at 7.00. Could you call me when he arrives?

Problems with the room

This key doesn't seem to work.

I have locked myself out.

My room has not been cleaned.

There are no towels.

Could I have an extra pillow please?

Could I have a quieter room?

Would it be possible to change room, it's very noisy?

Checking out

I'd like to pay my bill.

I haven't used anything from the minibar. But I did make one phone call.

I'll be paying by Visa.

The bill should have already been paid by my company.

I think there is a mistake here - I didn't have anything from the bar.

Could I have my passport back?

Can I leave my luggage here and collect it later?

I left you a case this morning.

No it's not that one, it's got a blue stripe on it. Yes, that one.

Could you ring for a taxi for me?

14.14 Telephoning

Saying who you are

Good morning this is Hai Li, from the Chinese Institute of …

Hello this is Manjula Whulanza. I'm calling from the University of Indonesia.

Saying who you want to speak to

Could I speak to Professor Williams please?

Yes, of course, I'll just put you through.

I'm sorry but she is not available at the moment.

Well, if Professor Williams is not in, could I speak to her secretary / assistant?

Could you put me through to Dr Heinrich Muller please?

Asking who you are speaking to

Sorry, who am I speaking to?

This is Professor William's assistant.

This is Carol on reception.

Is that Dr Abdelwahab?

Yes, speaking.

Explaining where you got their number from

Your name was given to me by Dr Bhattacharjee, who thought you …

I got your number from your department's website. I hope I am not disturbing you.

If you remember we met at the conference last week. I am the student from Bhutan and you gave me your phone number …

Speaking to someone you already know

Hello. This is Vladimir speaking.

Good morning. This is Vladimir Ancherbak speaking.

Hi Josefina, this is Ivan, how are you?

Hey, Ivan, good to hear from you. I'm fine thanks and you?

Giving reason for your call

I'm calling about …

The reason I'm calling is to find out if you …

I wonder if you can help me.

Could you tell me whether … ?

Explaining more about yourself to someone who does not know you

My name is Jacqueline Belchev and I am a postdoc student at …

I read your paper on … and I was wondering whether …

I came to your presentation on … and I have a couple of questions to ask regarding …

Spelling out names and numbers

Could you ask her to ring me back on 02 878 705 (zero two / eight seven eight / seven zero five).

I'm sorry but I gave you the wrong number. It's two one six, not two three six.

Shall I spell that for you?

I'll spell that again for you.

No, there is only one B in Weber not two.

That's seventeen—one seven.

No, that's Rosi with an "i" not an "a".

Yes, that's right.

Asking for and giving email / website address

Could you give me your / his email address please?

Her address is: ana_regina at hotmail dot com. That's Ana with one N, A-N-A underscore regina at …

Is that one word or two?

His address is adrianwallwork at yahoo dot com. That's adrianwallwork all one word with no dots.

The website is: e4ac.com / books, that's the letter E as in Ecuador, then the number four as a digit, then the letters A and C, then dot com, then slash "books."

Is that A as in Argentina?

Is that a forward slash?

Ending call

OK. Thanks for your help. Goodbye.

Problems with the line and mobile phone reception

The line's very faint / bad.

Do you think you could call me back? I can hardly hear you.

Would you mind calling me back? The line is terrible.

I think I'd better call you back. The line is terrible.

Sorry the reception is not very good here.

Sorry you're breaking up.

Sorry I am just about to go through a tunnel so we may get cut off.

I'm so sorry we got cut off.

Problems with voice and speed

Do you think you could speak up a little, please?

Could you speak a little more slowly please?

Talking on Skype

Can you see me OK now?

Do you want me to turn on / off the video?

I don't think you've got your microphone on properly.

I can hear you but I can't see you.

I can only see your feet / desk at the moment.

Do you think you could upload the document?

I have just sent you a chat message, did you get?

Could you write that down for me and send it as a message—thanks.

Sorry, for some reason we got cut off.

Sorry, someone else seems to be trying to call me, can you just hang on a second?

Saying goodbye

OK / Right, I think that's all.

Well, I think that's everything. Goodbye.

I look forward to seeing you.

Do call if you need anything else.

Have a nice day / weekend.

Hear from you soon. Bye.

Chapter 15

Mini Grammar and Frequently Confused Words List

❖ English is virtually the only language in the world that uses the present perfect to say *I have been here for three days* to indicate that *I arrived here three days ago and I am still here*. Most other languages use the present.

❖ English is probably only language where the word *actually* means *in fact* and not *at the moment*. However, the English meaning is closest to the original Latin meaning.

❖ Some languages have no articles, no verb *to have* (e.g. Welsh), no prepositions, and even no tenses.

❖ The English language is constantly changing. Until quite recently these plural forms of what were original countable nouns, would have been considered unacceptable: *accommodations, feedbacks, homeworks, softwares*. The use of the definite article (*the*) is getting less and less.

❖ Word order varies massively from language to language. Here are the equivalents of "I like you": *Like to me you* (Croatian), *You like to me* (Estonian), *I you like* (Korean), *To me you like* (Spanish), *You me I like* (Wolof).

❖ A German, an Italian (and all Latinate languages) and an Arab will say *I want that you go* rather than *I want you to go*. In other languages such as Polish, Russian and Estonian the literal translation will often be *I want you go*. In English it is: *I want you to go*.

❖ What do English as a foreign language teachers find hard to explain to their students? The difference between: the present perfect and the simple past, *that* vs *which*, *try and do* vs *try to do*, the genitive ('s), and exactly how phrasal verbs work. Are they really worth explaining? Only the first two.

❖ Examples given in grammar books can be quite intriguing. Here are some from a Chinese book on typical errors made by Chinese students, published in 1999: "He felt painless when he was tortured by the enemy because he was thinking of the nation and not of himself." "The colonialists thought by doing so could they trample on the democracy of the African peoples." "We are studying hard so that we can serve for the people in future." "The Chinese people resisted eight years for opposing to the Japanese aggressor".

❖ In some rural and urban areas of the US and UK, the majority of people do not use the 's' of the third person, and thus say *he come, she go* etc.

© Springer International Publishing Switzerland 2016
A. Wallwork, *English for Interacting on Campus*,
English for Academic Research, DOI 10.1007/978-3-319-28734-8_15

198

15.1 What's the buzz?

1) Answer the quiz and discuss with the class (this exercise is not for self-study).

To what extremes would you go to improve your English?   YES   NO   MAYBE

1. Spend all your spare money on English courses
2. Do expensive 1:1 English lessons with a private teacher
3. Spend half the weekend studying English
4. Get satellite TV, Netflix etc to watch programs in English
5. Talk only in English with my friends
6. Go to university in an English speaking country
7. Marry a native English speaker
8. Go on English speaking chatlines
9. Watch English teaching videos five hours a day
10. Have your tongue surgically modified so that you have perfect pronunciation

2) Write the correct version of the numbered items in this dialog between and English teacher and a *student*.

Good morning.

Sorry for the late! 1

How are you?

Well. (Pause) Am I only today? 2

No I think the others are coming.

What day is today? 3

It's Thursday.

Please? 4

It's Thursday.

How is written Thursday? 5

T-H-U-R-S-D-A-Y. *(Pause)* Is Carla here today?

A moment I control. (Goes and returns) She's arriving. 6

OK. Let's start anyway. Can you turn to page 66?

I have forgotten my book at house. 7

Well did you do the exercises I gave you?

I have not understood what you have said me. 8

I said: did you do the exercises I gave you?

Excuse me but I haven't made the lesson for home. 9

OK, well here you are. *(Teacher gives Student a photocopy)*

Have I to read? 10

No, just write the answers.

Repeat please. 11

No you don't have to read it, you only need write the answers.

A question. What does it means the number two? 12

It means .....

(Student completes the exercise). So what are you going to do this weekend?

Nothing of special. I relax myself. 13

Well have a nice weekend anyway.

Also to you. (Pause) Sorry. I cannot participate to the lesson of Monday. Will be the second lesson I lose this month. 14

OK. See you next Thursday then.

(leaving the class): Hi! 15

Where's my valium?

3) Two students, who have just met, are chatting to each other. Nearly every sentence contains a mistake - find the mistakes and correct them.

1. Where you live?

2. *I stay in the historical centre, we have the home at the fifth floor.*

3. You practise any sports?

4. *Yes.*

5. Which sports do you prefer?

6. *I like very much football.*

7. Also I like football. Have you seen the match this night?

8. *Yes, according to me the Italy had to win.*

9. I am agree with you.

10. *What type of studies do you do?*

11. I frequent the university. I am graduating in languages. I understand little.

12. *How many time are you at university?*

13. I am studying since two years. After the degree I find a work.

14. *Where have you passed the holidays the last year?*

15. I went in mountain and after to the sea, and then to my village.

16. *Did you stay well? With who you went?*

17. We went I and my girlfriend. We found a wonderful weather. There was few persons in beach so we enjoyed very much.

18. *Talk me of the your girl.*

19. She has 18 years. She is tall one meter and eighty. She has the green eyes. Actually she does the part time in a society.

20. *The next lesson you must to take me the photos of her. Have you the digital camera?*

21. Yes, I have it. *(Pause)* You speak a better English of me.

22. *You joke! I don't know nothing of English, also if I study since when I am baby.*

23. If you will study on this new book there is the possibility that you learn in a way better.

24. *I think yes. You have right! We see each other early I hope.*

25. I hope it also me.

KEY

Ex 2 1 Sorry I'm late. 2 Am I alone today? / Is it just me today? 3 What day is it today? 4 Sorry? 5 How do you spell Thursday? 6 Just a moment/sec I'll go and check. Yes, she's coming. 7 I left my book at home. 8 I didn't understand what you said. 9 I didn't do / haven't done the homework 10 Do you want me to read aloud? Shall I read aloud? Do I have to read aloud? 11 Sorry? / What did you say? / Could you say that again? 12 Can I just ask a question? What does number two mean? 13 Nothing special. I'm just going to relax. 14 The same to you. / You too. Sorry but I can't come / won't be able to come to Monday's lesson / the lesson on Monday. It will be the second lesson I have missed this month. 15 Bye. / Goodbye.

Ex 3 1 Where do you live? 2 I live in the old part of town / medieval quarter, we have a flat on the fifth floor. 3 Do you play any sports? 4 Yes (I do). 5 Which sports do you like (the most)? 6 I like football very much. / I really like football. 7 I like football too. Did you see/watch the match last night? 8 Yes, I thought Italy should have won. 9 I agree with you. 10 Are you at university? / What do you study? 11 I am at university. I am doing a degree in languages. I don't understand very much. 12 How long have been at university? 13 I have been studying for two years. After I've graduated / When I have got my degree I will look for / try and find a job. 14 Where did you go on holiday last year? 15 I went to the mountains and then to the sea, and then to my parents / my hometown / the place where I come from. 16 Did you have a good time? Who did you go with? 17 I went with my girlfriend. The weather was wonderful. There weren't many people on the beach so we enjoyed ourselves a lot / we had a really good time / we had a lot of fun. 18 Tell me about your girlfriend.. 19 She is 18 (years old). She is one meter eighty tall. She has (got) green eyes. At the moment she's working part time for a company. 20 Next lesson you must bring me some photos of her. Do you have / Have you got a digital camera? 21 Yes, I do. / Yes, I have one. (Pause) You speak better English than me. 22 You are joking! / You must be joking. I don't know any English, even though I've been studying since when I was a child. 23 If you study this new book you may learn better. 24 I think so. You are right! See you soon I hope. 25 I hope so too.

******

This chapter outlines a few important grammar items along with some pairs / triplets of words that are frequently confused. It is NOT comprehensive. For a more comprehensive guide to English grammar as used when writing research papers, see the companion volume *English for Research: Grammar, Style and Usage.*

15.2   Adverbs – position of

Don't put an adverb between a verb and its object.

I want to go *very much* (end position)

I *very much* want to go. (mid position)

Adverbs can go in three positions, depending on their type.

1) at the beginning of the clause: connecting adverbs (e.g. anyway, but, however), time adverbs (e.g. yesterday, last week). However, time adverbs can also go at the end.

Last Monday we went to Paris. or: We went to Paris *last Monday*.

2) in the middle of the clause (i.e. between the subject and the verb, or between the auxiliary and the verb/past participle; but after the verb to be in the present and past): adverbs of frequency (e.g. often, sometimes, never), certainty (e.g. certainly, surely, definitely), completeness (e.g. almost, nearly).

He'll *definitely* be here soon.

She is *often* late for lesson.

3) at the end of the clause: adverbs of manner (e.g. quickly, unwillingly), place (e.g. outside, upstairs) and time; also adverbs of frequency made up two or more words (this afternoon, three times a month).

15.3   Articles

Specific vs non specific

We use *a/an* to mean 'any'. If I say *have you got a pen?* it means any pen, it's not important which one. When the object is already known or when we specify which one we use 'the', e.g. *have you got the pen I lent you yesterday*.

When the object is part of our particular world or realm of interest we use *the*. If I say *I've got to go to the bank*, I am referring to my usual bank. If I talk about *the government*, I refer to the government in my country. *If I say don't stay out in the sun*, I am talking about something unique, the sun above us. But when we talk about something generic we use *a/an*, e.g. *a good bank shouldn't charge you more than 5% interest* or *a government should look after its citizens.*

Classes of objects and people

If we talk about a class of objects in an abstract sense we use the, but in a definition we usually prefer *a/an.*

The computer has changed the way we live.
A computer is an essential item. A computer is a machine which performs calculations.
We use *the* before an adjective to describe a class of people:
The rich are getting richer and the poor poorer.

General statements

No article is used when we make general statements about objects that have not been specified or mentioned before.

Apples are good for you. (but: I've put the apples in the fridge).
Life is for living. (but: The life of Shakespeare is very interesting).
It may not be clear what is and is not specific, but generally if a noun is followed by *of* it will be preceded by the. Compare:
Life in the middle ages was hard.
The life of a peasant in the the middle ages was hard.

Adjectives don't necessarily make their noun specific e.g. *I prefer red wine to white wine.* But *the red wine we tasted last night*, is specific, I can answer the question 'which red wine?'.

Other cases where *the* is not used

Below are some of the most common cases where *the* is not used, for other uses consult a good grammar.

1) languages

I speak English, Chinese and Dutch.

2) nationalities that do not end in *–ese, –ch, –sh*

Italians do it better.
The French drink more wine than the Portuguese.

If we have a sentence with both types of nationality then we tend to use *the* in both cases.

The French drink more wine than the Italians.

3) *bed, church, college, hospital, prison, school, university* and *work*

When we use the above in their primary sense we don't use the article.

I went to hospital to have an operation. (I was a patient).
I went to the hospital to see my mother who had had an operation. (I was a visitor)

But:

I went to the cinema, the restaurant, the bank.

4) geographical places

Asia, France, Mount Everest

But places that contain any of the following words in their name take *the*: Union, Kingdom, Republic, Sea, Ocean, Gulf, Pole, River and Isle. The is also used with names of deserts (the Sahara) and mountain ranges (the Alps), plural place names (the Netherlands) and before expressions like the West, the Middle East, the Third World.

5) certain fixed expressions

have breakfast, make progress, by car, on time

But: play the piano, listen to the radio

6) with possessives and parts of the body

I've read your book.
My head hurts.

But: I was hit in the head. (passive actions)

15.4   Comparisons

Use the comparative form (*more, better, worse*) to compare two things:

The system performed better / worse / more efficiently in the first test than in the second test.

Use the superlative form (*most, best, worst*) to describe something in absolute terms

The application returns only the most relevant results.
It always chooses the best solution.

Note the use of:

than not *then* or *of* when comparing two things or people

The first is better than the second.

as not *of* with *the same*

The first is the same as the second.

as ... as in comparatives that highlight the similarity between things (in both affirmative and negative sentences

The first is as good as the second.
The first is not as good as the second.

15.5   Conditionals

There are basically four types of conditional, though combinations of all four are also possible in relation to how one action/event depends on another.

Zero conditional (if + present + present)

Expresses general truths and scientific facts. It means 'every time that' or 'whenever'.

If you mix black and white you get grey.
In this department the professors don't really mind if you arrive late to lectures.

First conditional (if + present + will)

Expresses statements about the real world, but about particular actions/events now or in the future, rather than general truths which are always valid.

> If you're not careful you'll break it.
> Will you tell her if you see her?

Second conditional (if + past simple + would)

Expresses ideas which are not real at the moment and which perhaps could never be real.

> If I were/was you, I would tell her. (I am not you)
> If I studied more and partied less I'd probably pass more exams. (I am addicted to partying)

Third conditional (if + past perfect + would have + past participle)

Expresses how things might have been if something had (not) happened. It can be used to express regrets and hypotheses about the past, missed opportunities and criticisms of oneself or others.

> If I had known it was going to cause such problems, I would never have told her.
> Wouldn't it have been better if you had done it the other way round?

Mixed conditionals

You can mix the different forms as required.

> If it hadn't been for you, I wouldn't be here now.
> If you wanted it a different colour you should have told me when you ordered it.

15.6   Countable vs uncountable nouns

An uncountable noun is a noun that you cannot count or make plural. For example, you cannot say a water, one water, two waters, a thousand waters. Sometimes it is clear which nouns are impossible to count, but not always. The following are some of the most common uncountable nouns in everyday English:

> *advice, apparatus, business, capital, chewing gum, entertainment, equipment, expertise, furniture, feedback, gold (and other metals), hardware, help, income, inflation, information, intelligence, luck, knowhow, knowledge, luggage, machinery, money, news, permission, progress, research, software, traffic, transport, work*

To make them countable we use *some/any* (e.g. I'd like some information, have you got any accommodation?), *a bit of* (can I give you a bit of advice?), *a piece of* (you're allowed one piece of hand luggage) or *a means of* (a means of transport).

Some nouns can be both countable or uncountable (e.g. coffee, glass, interest, material, paper), but their meaning changes. For example:

I love coffee.
Can I have two coffees. (i.e. cups of coffee)

Others can be preceded by the indefinite article if they are accompanied with an adjective:

A good knowledge of English.

Some nouns that until recently were considered uncountable are *feedback* and *homework*, however these are now often used in a plural form particularly in the USA.

Quantifiers

Below is a list of quantifiers. Unless otherwise specified they can be used with both countable (C) and uncountable (U) nouns:

a bit of (U), a few (C), a great deal of, a huge amount of, a large amount of, a little (U), a lot of, a number of , all, each, enough, every, few (C), hardly any, little (U), lots of, many (C), masses of, most, nearly all, none / not any, not many (C), not much (C), plenty of (= a sufficient amount of), quite a few (C), quite a lot of, several (C), some.

much and *many* tend to be used in negatives, and *a lot of* and *lots of* in affirmatives; in interrogatives all of them can be used.

I haven't got much time.
Have you got many / a lot of books by Stephen King?
Do you have much / a lot of interest in this?

a little and *a few* are the equivalent of some, whereas *little* and *few* mean *hardly any:*

I know a few people who can speak Dutch.
I know few people in Europe who can speak Swahili.

any is generally used in negatives and interrogatives, and *some* in affirmatives. *Some* is also used in interrogatives when these are offers and requests:

Would you like some more beer?
Can I have some milk please?

some can also be used in negatives.

> I didn't answer some of the questions (= I answered some but not all)
> I didn't answer any of the questions (= I didn't answer a single question)

plenty means more than a sufficient number of, *enough* means sufficient but not excessive. *Plenty* is generally used in response to what someone else has just said.

> Don't worry! We've got plenty of time – the train doesn't leave for five hours.
> We've got just enough time to get there – the train leaves in half an hour.

15.7   Future forms

The tense we choose for the future relates more to our attitude towards the event rather than time. So the tense/structure will depend on our and other people's intentions, on how certain we are that something will happen, and on how much control we have over what will happen; it also depends on the type of verb we use (state or action). It is important to note that in many cases more than one tense can be used, often with no real difference in meaning.

Predictions, giving/asking for info (present simple, will, going to, future continuous, future perfect)

Use WILL to predict, guess, or calculate what you think will happen. In the affirmative it is often used with as a statement of fact or for official events (the PRESENT SIMPLE can often be used too). SHALL can be used in the first person, but generally the contracted form ('ll) is used.

> Who do you think will win the match?
> When do / will you get your results?
> Next term begins / will begin on September 13.
> I'm sure they won't get it done on time.

When we have external evidence or support for what we are saying (i.e. there are already clear signs) we often used the GOING TO form, particularly when we give warnings and advice, whereas WILL has a more intuitive value. Compare:

> Be careful! You're going to break it. (you're handling the object now)
> Don't give it to the baby, she'll only break it. (based on your knowledge of children)

The FUTURE CONTINUOUS is used for actions that are going on now and which we think will progress into the future.

I wonder if they'll still be studying or if they've already gone home.

The FUTURE CONTINUOUS is also used when we project ourselves into the future and see something happening.

This time next week we'll be lying under the sun in Tenerife.
In a few minutes we shall be arriving at La Guardia airport.

We use the FUTURE PERFECT when we project ourselves into the future and look back to say whether an action has been completed.

Will you have finished writing up the report by the time I get back?

The FUTURE PERFECT is also used to speculate about the present.

Do you think they will have left by now or will they still be at home?

Intentions (will, going to, present continuous, future continuous)

We use WILL to make spontaneous decisions as a reaction to events that have just happened.

My mobile's ringing, can someone answer it for me please? OK, I'll get it.
What would you like to drink? I'll have a beer please.

In the negative WILL usually indicates a refusal to do something.

He can say what he likes, but I won't speak to him ever again.
The computer won't turn on.

We use GOING TO when we have already taken a decision but we haven't necessarily made any final plans.

I'm going to buy the new iPhone but I still haven't decided which model yet.
I hear you're going to sell your bike, have you found a buyer?
Are you going to carry on using the computer or can I turn it off?

The PRESENT CONTINUOUS is used when our plans have been finalised, when all the arrangements and agreements have been made.

Next summer we're traveling round Europe by train.

We generally also use the PRESENT CONTINUOUS when we ask people about their plans for this evening, the weekend or the holidays, even if no definite arrangements have been made.

Are you doing anything interesting this weekend?
Where are they going on holiday this year?

The PRESENT CONTINUOUS is usually only used with verbs of movement, with other verbs GOING TO is used. Compare:

What are you doing tonight? I'm going to study / read / watch TV.
What are you doing tonight? I'm playing tennis with Clare then we're going to the cinema.

When we want to talk about a future that will take place independently of our own volition and intentions (or we want it to seem like this), we use the FUTURE CONTINUOUS.

Ms Southern will be arriving on the 6.0 flight, if you could make all the necessary arrangements.
If you want a lift to the airport I'll be going there myself, I've got to pick up Anna there.
I'm afraid I won't be coming into work today, I've got a very bad cough and cold. (compare: I won't come into work = I refuse to come)

Using the future continuous is thus a polite way to ask other people about their intentions without trying to influence them.

Will you be needing any more help with this, or can I go home now?
Will you be seeing Olaf next week, if so could you give him this?

15.8 Gerund vs infinitive

1 The gerund is used when the verb is the subject of the sentence, the infinitive when talking about objectives.

Cooking is a wonderful past time.
To cook well you need years of practice.

2 All verbs followed by a preposition, particle or adverb automatically take the gerund:

Shall we carry on doing this?
I don't feel like eating anything.
I can't put off going.

3 Some of the most common verbs followed by the gerund (and never by the infinitive) are: *avoid, can't help, dislike, enjoy, entail, finish, involve, mean, mind, miss, practise, prevent, recall, resist*

4 The following verbs can be used with either the gerund or the infinitive with little or no change in meaning: *begin, bother, cause, continue, hate, intend, like, love, prefer, start*. However, with *hate, like, love* and *prefer* we cannot use the gerund with the conditional form (*I would love to go*).

5 Some verbs change meaning depending on whether they are followed by the gerund or the infinitive.

When you *stop doing something* it means that you no longer do it. Whereas if you *stop to do something*, you interrupt one activity in order to start another.

> I stopped smoking last year.
> We stopped the car to check the engine.

If I do not *remember doing something* it means I have no recollection of the event. Whereas if I don't *remember to do something* it simply means that I forgot.

> I don't remember having said anything at all compromising.
> Don't worry. This time I'll remember to tell them – I won't forget again.

If you regret doing something, you have already done it and you're sorry about it. If you regret to have to do something, it refers to something in the future.

> I regret telling him about my previous relationships.
> I regret to tell you that we are closing down this office.

6 Certain verbs - *hear, listen to, see, watch, look at, notice* and *feel* can be used either with the infinitive without to or with the gerund. The infinitive describes a complete action from beginning to end, the gerund describes an action that had already begun and was continuing at a particular moment.

> I heard her play one of Bach's sonatas. (I heard the whole piece)
> I heard her playing the violin. (I was outside the door and didn't go in to hear everything)

15.9   Have/get something done

The construction *to have something* + past participle has two meanings.

1) to say that someone does something for you

I had my eyes tested by the optician.

2) to say that someone did something (generally unpleasant) to you that you didn't want them to do

She had her bicycle stolen.

get should be used instead of *have* on some occasions, particularly when you do something yourself.

Let's get the room cleaned before Richard comes home. (i.e. we will room the house not aks someone else to do it for us).
I must get my thesis finished – the deadline is next week. (i.e. I will finish the thesis).

15.10   Modal verbs

Obligation

must is used when you give someone a direct order to do something, so in this sense it is not used very often except when giving people strong advice/invitations or when there is a sense of urgency, *must* is not usually used in the interrogative form.

You must come at once there's been an accident.
You must come and see us next time you're in town.
The doctor says I mustn't smoke weed anymore.

Most of our obligations are imposed on us by other people or by external events/situations. In these cases we use *have to*. Note that *have to* is like a regular verb and no contractions are used, unless it is followed by *got*, so you *I have to* not *I've to*, and *do you have to?* and not *have you to?*. *will have to* and not *must* is used to refer to the future,

In most countries in Europe you have to wear a helmet if you use a motorbike.
I have to get up at six most mornings.
I think I'll have to get a new smart phone – this one's getting out of date.

Note that *don't have to* indicates an absence of obligation, it means *don't need to*, it's not necessary. *must*, on the other hand, indicates an obligation not to do something.

> I don't have to get up at six anymore because I don't need to be at college until 9.00 now.
> You mustn't eat with your mouth open.

If you think it is/was a good idea to do something, or if there is some moral obligation involved, then use *should* or *should have* + past participle.

> You should really see your mother more often.
> You should have told me you were coming, I would have made a meal.

If there is an obligation to do something, but we don't respect this obligation, then we use *be supposed to*.

> We were supposed to be there at six, but we actually arrived at 9.30.
> You are supposed to be responsible for this project, why haven't you done anything?

must is not used to express obligation in the past, instead we use *have to* which indicates a past obligation that was respected.

> I had to go to a conference in Georgia last week, it was a really interesting trip.

Ability and permission

can (present) and *could* (past) are used to talk about a general ability and permission to do something.

> I can swim. I could swim when I was six.
> We can / could do whatever we like. (= we are / were allowed to)

can is not used to talk about future ability (unless we are deciding now to do something). When talking about an ability to do something on one particular occasion, *could* is not used in the affirmative and interrogative forms. In both these cases we use a form of *to be able to* or *manage*. However, to talk about any cases of permission, either on one occasion or in general, we can use *could* in all forms.

> I will be able to swim better when I've finished my lesson. (ability, not: I can swim)
> I was able to pass the test. (ability, not: I could)
> Did you manage to pass the test? (ability, not: could you?)
> I could only answer two of the questions. (alternatively: I was only able ..)

Could you / Were you allowed to eat whatever you wanted? (permission, both possible)

Couldn't you get / Weren't you allowed in to the museum? (permission, both possible)

Speculating and predicting, possibility and probability

can is used to talk about a general possibility or to say that something is quite typical.

You can start now or begin in a couple of weeks if you prefer.
It can rain a lot in Manchester.

However, when you talk about the actual chances of something happening, use *may* or *might* (slightly less probable).

We may start this month or next, I'm not sure.
It might rain when we're in Manchester next week.

To predict future possibilities you can also use *be possible / likely*.

It is unlikely that he'll be here before six. (= He's unlikely to be here before six.)

When making logical deductions about the present or past *can* is not used in the affirmative.

Who's that at the door? It may / might / could be Priscilla.
Where are they? Well, they may / might have missed the train.

If we want to show certainty then we use *must* and *can't*.

It must be very difficult to learn Chinese in a month.
It can't have been Joe you saw – he's in Mongolia.

could / might have + past participle is used to say what was possible but didn't happen.

You shouldn't have driven so fast you could / might have had an accident.

15.11 Passive form

To form the passive, put the verb *to be* into the same tense as the active verb and add the past participle. For example:

> They are building a new road. (present continuous)
> A new road is being built. (present continuous of *to be* + past participle)

We use the passive when:

1) Our main interest is not in who or what carried out the actions; the most important item is the subject of the sentence:

> These shoes were made in Italy. (it is of little interest exactly who made the shoes)

2) It is unnecessary, difficult, or impossible to identify the originator of the action

> Several attempts have been made to convert stone into gold.

3) We are writing scientific report; though it may be much clearer and direct to use the active form:

> The results were compared with those of Alvarez.
> more direct: We compared our results with those of Alvarez.

4) We report what is commonly believed to be true:

> Larry Page is said to be quite a modest man despite being one the richest men in the world.
> The law is expected to be passed next month.

15.12   Past forms

The tense we choose for expressing past concepts depends very much on their relation to the present events (i.e. is there still a connection?), to other past events (i.e. is one past event dependent on another past event?), and to whether the actions only happened once, were repeated or were continuous at a particular moment.

Past and present (past simple, present perfect, present perfect continuous)

Both the PAST SIMPLE AND the PRESENT PERFECT can be used for completed actions.

> I've finished my assignment so I'm going to watch TV now.
> I think he finished his assignment before he went out.

The difference is that the PRESENT PERFECT strongly relates to a present situation. However, deciding what this connection is, is really quite complex. Use the PRESENT PERFECT

1) When you can see the result now:

> Who has drunk all my wine?
> Why are you looking so sad. What's happened?

2) When you are giving news:

> The government has put up the price of petrol again.
> I've passed my driving test.

3) When a (further related) action could still take place within a specific time frame:

> I've already made 10 phone calls this morning. (said at 10.00, I can still make more calls)
> I made 12 calls this morning. (said at 15.00, it's now the afternoon)

Note that when we use the PRESENT PERFECT we are normally more interested in <u>what</u> happened (focus on the result) than <u>when</u> it happened (focus on the action). But when we move on to the details (*when? why? who? where? how?*) we use the SIMPLE PAST.

> I've passed my driving test.
> Really, when did you take it? Was it difficult? How did you feel when they told you that you'd passed? Did you think you'd pass it?

The PRESENT PERFECT is also used to talk about experiences that took place at any unspecified time before now. It is thus used with adverbs such as ever, never, already, yet, recently, in the last few, in your life.

> I've had a lot of experience in this field. I've studied with computers, I've collaborated with various software houses, and I've travelled extensively throughout Europe.

But when we mention specific times in the past we use the SIMPLE PAST.

> When I first arrived at university I had no friends at all.

We use the PRESENT PERFECT CONTINUOUS to focus on the process of an action, which may or may not still be continuing. The PRESENT PERFECT looks at a result (which may be either intermediary or final). This means that the CONTINUOUS is not used with numbers (except in time expressions). Compare:

> Share prices have been rising for the last three months..
> Share prices have risen 26 points in the last two weeks.
> She's been drinking that's why she can hardly walk.
> She's drunk two bottles already, I think she should stop.

The PRESENT PERFECT CONTINUOUS cannot be used for actions that have no sense of progression. Compare:

> Damn! I've cut my finger. (momentary action, immediate completion and result)
> He's been cutting the grass all morning. (prolonged action)

The PRESENT PERFECT CONTINUOUS cannot usually be used for actions that took place at an indefinite time, the action must either have just finished or be still continuing. Compare:

> Have you ever seen Gone With The Wind?
> I've just been watching this great film – it's really good.

Sometimes both tenses can be used with little change in meaning, though the PRESENT PERFECT CONTINUOUS may focus on the temporary nature of the action.

> I've lived here nearly all my life. (almost permanent situation)
> I've only been living here a few weeks. (transitory situation)

Past habits (past simple, *used to*)

1 The PAST SIMPLE is used in much the same way as the present simple, i.e. to describe states and habits.

I lived in Estonia for five years before I moved to Latvia.
Before she retired, my mother was a lawyer.

2 We use USED TO when show how circumstances have changed.

This theatre used to be a factory.
I used to work 12 hours a day (but now I only work 8 hours)

3 You can't use USED TO when you say what happened at a past time, or the length and number of times involved.

I saw three films last week. (not: I used to see)
I went to the cinema six times last month. (not: I used to go)

Progress and background (past simple, past continuous)

1) The PAST CONTINUOUS gives a descriptive background to a narrative, whereas the PAST SIMPLE describes a state/habit or sequence of events. Compare:

She was wearing a blue dress and carrying an umbrella.
She generally wore a suit to work and always carried an umbrella.
I was leaving the room when she came in. (I had already decided to leave).
I left the room when she came in. (She had a direct influence on my decision)

2) The PAST CONTINUOUS is thus used to describe something in progress at a particular moment or when something else happened.

I phoned you at nine last night, but there was no reply. Yes, sorry I was having a bath.

3) The PAST CONTINUOUS can also be used to stress that an activity was in progress throughout a complete period. Compare:

I was studying all yesterday and Heinz was cooking for most of the day.
I studied in the morning, then went out.

4) As with the future continuous the PAST CONTINUOUS can be used to make requests more polite.

I was wondering if you could help me write this assignment.

The past in the past (past simple, past perfect, past perfect continuous)

1) When we are talking about the past and we need to emphasise that action A happened even earlier than action B, then we use the PAST PERFECT. Compare:

They had already left when we arrived. (first they left, then we arrived)
They left when we arrived. (contemporary actions)
I left my car to be serviced this morning – is it ready yet? (only one past action)
Had you seen the film before and is that why you didn't want to do again? (explanation)
Did you see the film before you went to the restaurant or after? (sequence of events)

2) The PAST PERFECT is often used with verbs like *realise, think, wonder* and *say*.

Did you think you had already told me?
We realised we had made a terrible mistake.

3) The PAST PERFECT and PAST PERFECT CONTINUOUS are often simply the past forms of the present perfect and present perfect continuous. Compare:

This is the first time I have been here.
It was the first time I had been there.
He has been studying all day – that's why he is so tired.
He had been studying all day – that's why he was so tired.

15.13   Phrasal verbs

The English language is constantly creating new phrasal verbs, i.e. a base verb + a preposition or adverb. Because they are so widespread it is useful to be able to recognise the most common ones, though you can in fact communicate quite easily without ever using more than 20 or so of them. The rules are exceptionally complicated, especially because they vary depending on whether the verb is followed by a preposition or an adverb (which is not easy to decide). For further information consult a good grammar or learner's dictionary.

In verb + preposition/s combinations, never put the object before the preposition.

I'll carry on with it. not I'll carry it on with

In verb + adverb combinations, nouns or short phrases can come either at the end or after the adverb, longer phrases after the adverb, and pronouns come before the adverb.

Can you *sort out* the arrangements?

Can you *sort* the arrangements *out*?
Can you *sort out* the arrangements for next week's lectures and presentations?
Can you *sort* them *out*? not ~~Can you sort out them~~?

In any case, don't fixate about phrasal verbs. With a few exceptions, it is possible to avoid them completely.

15.14   Present forms

1 The PRESENT SIMPLE describes permanent regular features of our life and our environment, whereas the PRESENT CONTINUOUS is used for temporary features, trends or things that are happening now.

His parents live in Santiago.
He's living with me until he finds accommodation on campus.
The cost of living is rising rapidly at the moment.
The cost of living rises every year.

2 The PRESENT SIMPLE is used for official timetables and schedules, the PRESENT CONTINUOUS is used for personal plans (though the present simple would be used for a complete itinerary).

There are trains from this station every 15 minutes. The next one leaves at 3.15.

I'm leaving on the 3.15 to Copenhagen. Then I change in Copenhagen and take the 5.26 to Malmo.

3 If we want to describe something that is a habit or state in the present but relate it back to the past we use the PRESENT PERFECT SIMPLE rather than the PRESENT SIMPLE. Compare:

She is an assistant professor.
She has been assistant professor for three years.

4 Likewise we use the PRESENT CONTINUOUS with something happening now but with no relation to the past, where instead we use the PRESENT PERFECT CONTINUOUS. Compare:

She's living with us for the moment.
She's been living with us since last week.

5 Note that we use the PRESENT PERFECT SIMPLE, and not the PRESENT SIMPLE, in expressions such as "this is the first / second time …"

This is the first time I have eaten Chinese food. (i.e. I have never eaten Chinese food before)

15.15 Progressive vs simple vs perfect

Certain verbs do not take continuous forms, particularly those that refer something that doesn't change over time, rather than to physical and temporary actions. Examples:

1 verbs of the senses (e.g. *see, hear, smell, taste, feel*)

When these are used in their primary meaning they are often accompanied by *can*.

I can't see you. Can you hear?

However, they can be used in the continuous form but with a different meaning.

I'm seeing Pete tomorrow. (i.e. I have a meeting with him)
I've been hearing a lot from her recently (i.e. we've been in contact)

2 verbs of mental and emotional activity (e.g. *agree, believe, imagine, promise, realise, recognise, think*)

I couldn't / didn't understand what she was talking about.

However, *think* and *expect* can be used in the continuous but with a different meaning. Compare:

I expect you like tea since you're English. (= I imagine)
I'm expecting them at 9.0. (= we have an appointment)
What are you thinking about, you look rather sad. (= what's going on in your head)
What did you think about that new film? (= what's your opinion)

3 verbs of possession and measurement (e.g. *fit, suit, weigh, belong, possess, own, contain, consist*)

This laptop belongs to the prof. It contains all her data.

Perfect forms of a verb focus on how we see an event, either its connection to a later event but more particularly to its sense of completion in terms of its result.

15.16   Relative clauses

1) You will rarely make a mistake if you always use *who* for people and *which* for things. However, punctuation can be important – note the difference:

My brother who/that lives in Oslo is a musician.
My brother, who lives in Oslo, is a musician.

The first sentence is an identifying clause, so called because it identifies which brother I am talking about, i.e. I have more than one brother and in this case I'm talking about the one who lives in Oslo. The second sentence is a non- identifying clause, i.e. I only have one brother and the fact that he lives in Oslo is some additional but not essential information.

2) that can replace who and which in identifying clauses but not in non- identifying clauses.

This is the computer (that/which) I was telling you about.
He lives in Oslo, which is the capital of Norway.

3) We can omit the relative pronoun when it is not the subject of the sentence.

He's the professor (who/that) I am going to be doing my thesis under.

In this case I am the subject of the verb (*told*) not the professor.

4) In non- identifying clauses words and expressions such as *some, any, several, enough, most, a number, half, the majority*, can be used with *of whom* and *of which*.

I had a group of tourists none of whom spoke any English.
I've got hundreds of CDs most of which I never listen to.

5) Prepositions usually go to the end of the phrase, apart from in formal writing.

This is the proposal, with which I think you are acquainted. (very formal)
This is the proposal, which I think you are acquainted with. (very formal)

6) The possessive pronoun is whose, which is used for both people and things.

This is the man whose car was stolen.
This is the horse whose leg was broken.

7) In questions if who, which, whose or what are the subject of the sentence we don't use the auxiliaries do or did, only when they are the object.

Whose / Which horse won the race?
Whose / Which horse did you put your money on?
What happened next?
What did she say to you?

15.17   Reported speech

When we report someone's words we usually have to make certain changes (pronouns, adverbs of time), particularly with regard to the tense. If the reporting verb is in the present then we don't normally need to make any changes, but if the reporting verb is in the past changes may be necessary.

Mark: I've written the cards now I'll address the envelopes.
Mark *says* he *has* written the cards so now he *will* address the envelopes.
Mark *said* he *had* written the cards and that then he *would* address the envelopes.

The following tense changes are normally made:

TENSE	ORIGINAL WORDS	*She said that …*
Present Simple	"I work from 9 to 5."	.. she *studied* from 9 to 5.
Present Continuous	"I am studying till late tonight."	.. she *was studying* till late tonight.
Present Perfect	"I have been there twice."	.. she *had been* there twice.
Present perfect cont.	"I've been studying."	.. she *had been* studying.
Simple Past	"I lived there till 2016."	.. she *had lived* there till 2016.
Past cont.	"I was studying late."	.. she *had been* studying late.
Will	"I'll call back later."	.. she *would* call back later.
0 conditional	"If you mix X with Y you get Z"	.. if you *mix* X with Y you *get* Z.
1st conditional	"If you help me, I'll help you".	.. if he *helped* her she *would* help him.
2nd conditional	"I'd help you if I could."	.. she *would help* her if he could.
3rd conditional	"If I'd known I'd have done it"	.. she *had known* he *would have done* it.
can, may	"I can / may swim tomorrow"	.. she could / might swim.
must	"I must study tomorrow"	.. must / had to study tomorrow / the next day

15.18   Time clauses

The following adverbs *as soon as, when, while, after, before, until*, etc are immediately followed by the SIMPLE PRESENT or PRESENT PERFECT and not *will* (which goes in the other half of the clause).

> I'll call you when they come back.
> She says as soon as she has done it she'll let us know
> Note the difference between the meanings of these adverbs of time:

Use *by* to say that an action or event will happen at or before a certain future time, whereas *until* (or more informally, till) refers to a situation that will continue up to a particular moment. *while* has a similar meaning as until but is followed by a person rather than a time.

> I can do it from now until Friday, then I'll have to stop. (i.e. without interruption)
> I need it by Friday at the latest. (i.e. at any time before Friday)
> I'll need it while I am here.

15.19   Verbs + prepositions

Here are some common verbs with their related prepositions

agree	with	be reduced	to	consist	in/of
apologize	for	be representative	of	contrast	with
apply	for a job	be satisfied	with	cope	with
apply	to someone	be subject	to	count (=rely)	on
approve	of	belong	to	decide	on
associate	with	borrow	from	differ	from
be allergic	to	choose	from/	disapprove	of
be attached	to		between	discourage	from
be based	on	coincide	with	distinguish	between
be entitled	to	comment	on	dream	about
be fond	of	communicate	with		someone
be included	in	compare	to/with	dream	of doing
be inherent	in	compete	against/with		something
be intended	for	comply	with	exclude	from
be interested	in	concentrate	on	experiment	on
be involved	in	conflict	with	focus	on
be prejudiced	against	confuse	with	get accustomed	to

help	with	prevent (someone)	from	subscribe	to
hope	for			suffer	from
insure	against	protest	against	sympathize	with
listen	to	react	against/to	take part	in
look (=observe)	at	refer	to	taste	of
		rely	on	thank someone	for
look (=search)	for	reply	to		
look forward	to	respond	to	think	of/about
object	to	search	for	vote	for
participate	in	select	from	wait	for
pay (someone)	for	separate	from	warn	against/about

The following verbs take no preposition in their most common meanings: *tell, answer, discuss, study, investigate, call, phone, ask*

15.20   Frequently confused words

borrow, lend, loan

borrow means to take something from someone temporarily, whereas *lend* means to give someone something temporarily.

   Can I borrow this book (from you)?
   Could you lend this book to me? Could you lend me this book?

loan means the same as *lend* but is generally more formal.

   Libraries loan books, banks loan people money.

bring, take, carry, get, fetch, lead to

bring is associated with coming here (to where I am), whereas *take* with going there (away from me to somewhere else).

   Go home and take this with you.
   Remember to bring your books when you come to the lecture tomorrow.
   I've taken the PC to the repair shop.
   Thanks for the invite to your party - shall I bring some drinks?

carry means to transport in your arms or with your hands, it also refers to the physical capacity of some machines.

> She's the one who always carries the suitcases.
> This lift can carry up to 10 people.

get and *fetch* mean to go somewhere, collect something and then come back.

> Can you [go and] get my suit from the laundry?
> I'm just going to fetch the guys from the station.

lead to means to cause someone or something to go in a particular direction, both in a physical and figurative sentence.

> All roads lead to Rome.
> His strange behaviour led us to believe that he was severely depressed.

college, university

Both mean the same thing when someone says: *I go to college* or *When I graduate from university*.

However, a college can also be a way to divide up students in a university - they live, and often study, in different colleges around the campus (this is typical of Oxford and Cambridge universities in England).

do, make

Use *do* for i) generic activities ii) household jobs iii) academic activities.

> Did you do anything interesting at the weekend?
> What are you doing with that box?
> I do everything in this house: I do the shopping, I do the washing, I do the ironing, I do the shopping ...
> I haven't done my homework yet.
> I did my thesis on how taking selfies makes you selfish.
> We do research on genetics.

Use *do* in the following expressions: *business, favors, one's best, right, wrong, well, a job. Do* is not used with other countable nouns.

226

Use *make* i) when there is an end product ii) with mistakes and errors iii) with most countable nouns (*announcements, choices, proposals, suggestions* etc).

> These shoes are made in Italy.
> Can I make you a coffee?
> She didn't make any mistakes.
> I'll make you a proposal you can't refuse.

Use *make* with these uncountable nouns and expressions: *peace, love, money, progress, headway, a mess, sure, good, certain, the most of, fun of, room.*

> Make love not war.
> You've made a terrible mess.

NB *have*, rather than *make* or *do*, is used in the following cases: *a shower, a bath, breakfast, lunch, dinner*

earn, gain, win, beat

Both *earn* and *gain* mean to acquire. *earn* is generally used with money, *gain* with experience, time, and capital. Both verbs can be used with respect and a reputation.

> He's earned a lot of money playing poker.
> You need to gain some experience before we can promote you.

Win is used with objects (e.g. money, games), but *beat* with people.

> He won the game, in fact he beat me easily.

even though, even if

even though - for real situations. It can generally be replaced with *although*.

> Even though / Although the system is designed to work on PCs, it also works on Apple computers.

even if - for hypothetical situations and is generally followed by the simple past or past perfect

> Even if we had all the time in the world, we would never be able to finish the project.

job, work

job is a countable noun and means a paid occupation, or a task, duty or responsibility.

> He's got a job as an intern in a bank.
> We've got a lot of jobs to do today. We need to fix the computer, do those photo-copies and write up the report.
> It's not my job to clean up after your parties.
> Well done, you've done a really good job.

work is uncountable, so it's not possible to say *a work, one work*, or *works*. It refers to a mass of undefined tasks, or to one's place of occupation.

> Studying this astrophysics book is hard work.
> Things aren't going very well at work at the moment.

Sometimes both words could be used, with little or no change in meaning.

> Is the job/work interesting at the new place?
> What kind of job/work do you do?

(the) last, (the) next

last: the time before the current one (e.g. the week before the current week)

> Last lesson we talked about x, this lesson we are going to talk about y.

next: the time after current one (e.g. the year after the current year)

> We will be doing the test next week, on Monday in fact.

the last / the next: a specific time in the past or the future

> The last year that the Olympics were held in London was in 2012.

When you use *last* and *next* in conjunction with *weeks, months, years* (i.e. the plural form used to indicate a period), you must insert *few* before the time period.

> The last few years have seen a considerable rise in the number of …

lecture, lesson

A lecture is held in a lecture hall by a lecturer (who may be a professor, researcher, or even a PhD student) to a very large group of students. A lesson is held in a class-room to a group of around 20 students or less.

let, allow, permit, enable

All these verbs have the same meaning, though *let* is the least formal and *permit* the most formal. *enable* cannot be used when giving permission but only in the sense of facilitating. They all require a personal object when not used in the passive.

> The prof let us leave early from her lecture.
> They allowed/permitted us to leave early.
> This programme enables/permits/allows changes to be made.
> This programme lets you make changes.

let is less formal, requires the infinitive without *to*, and is not used in the passive form. The passive structure with it is only possible with *permit*, but is not very common.

> We were allowed/permitted to leave early.
> It is not permitted to smoke in this carriage. (Smoking is not permitted)

look, seem, sound

look, *seem* and *sound* can be directly followed by an adjective. If followed by a noun they are used with like, and before a verb they often followed by as if. *feel* and *taste* follow the same rules.

look is used for physical impressions and appearances

> You look tired today.
> He looks like his mother – he has the same expression.
> It looks as if it's going to rain

seem is used for intuitions and atmospheres

> Everyone was so happy, it seemed like a party.
> He doesn't seem to understand much.

sound relates to noises, someone's voice or to musical styles

> Listen. It sounds like a mouse.
> From what you've said your idea sounds really useful.

make vs let

make means force or oblige, *let* means allow or permit.

> Don't make me laugh.
> They made us do it even though we didn't want to.
> Please let me in.
> They let us see the church even though it was closed to the public.

miss, lose, waste

miss means to fail to be present or to be late when something happens, and so is usually used with transport, appointments and opportunities. *miss* is not used to say that someone hasn't got something.

> I've missed three lectures so far this month.
> We missed the first train so we had to catch the later one.
> Three people are missing on the mountain.
> I'm sorry but you're missing the point.

lose means not to have anymore. It is generally used with objects and money.

> I can't find my wallet I must have lost it.

waste means to consume unnecessarily.

> Don't waste time doing those exercises.
> He's wasted a lot of money buying useless objects.

rise, arise, raise

rise (rose, risen) is an intransitive verb and refers to involuntary actions (to go up, to reach a higher level).

> Last month the share index rose by 25 points.
> The sun rises in the east and sets in the west.

arise (arose, arisen) means the same as rise but in a figurative sense (to occur).

> I'm afraid that various problems have arisen.

raise is a transitive verb and refers to voluntary actions (to make higher, to propose, to lift).

> The government have raised taxes.
> She raised several points during the lecture.

professor, lecturer, supervisor, advisor, tutor

The academic hierarchy in the US is: assistant professors, associate professors or full professors. In the UK academics start their career as lecturers, then move to senior lecturer, and then finally to professor. A supervisor or advisor or tutor (generally all three with the same meaning), is the person who has been assigned to you to decide your research program and help you to organize your work and thesis. Your supervisor or advisor or tutor could be a lecturer or (assistant) professor.

say, tell

Use *say* to report or refer to the exact words someone used.

> He said: 'I adore you'
> She said 'goodbye' to me and then left.
> Sorry, what did you say?
> How do you say 'xxx' in English?
> Say what you think.

Use *tell* to report the contents of what of someone said, rather than the exact words that they used. It must be followed by a pronoun or person and is not followed by *to*.

> He told me that he adored me.
> What did you tell her to do?
> Tell me what you think.

sorry, afraid, apologize, excuse

> *Sorry* is used when you need to apologize for something small or for something in advance.
> Sorry I'm late.
> Sorry but I won't be able to come next week.
> Sorry, did I hurt you?

I'm afraid is used when you have to say something to someone that they may not like.

> I'm afraid I've got some bad news.

Use *excuse me* to apologize politely for disturbing or interrupting someone.

> Excuse me, but I just need to make a quick phone call.
> Excuse me, have you got the time please?

Say *'I apologize'* when you want to be quite formal.

> I must apologize for my behaviour last night.

speak, talk

Use *speak* in the following cases i) with languages ii) on the phone iii) to someone formally.

She speaks fluent Chinese.
This is Andrea Coli speaking. Could I speak to Anne Jobs please?
I'll speak to my prof and see what she says.
The President is speaking on the TV tonight.

Use *talk* in the sense of having an informal chat, conversation or discussion.

Sorry I can't talk to you now I'm really busy.
What did you talk about in the workshop?

travel, trip, journey

travel is generally a verb or adjective.

We traveled to Cuba via Miami, as recommended by the travel agent.

trip is used i) to specify a movement from a to b (similar meaning to *journey*) ii) to specify the movement and what you did there.

The whole trip lasted just over two hours.
Did you have a good trip to Cuba?

journey means exclusively the time you spent traveling.

The journey was a nightmare, it took over ten hours.

watch, look at, see

Use *watch* for things that are moving (people, images on film, shows).

Aren't you going to watch TV tonight?
Watch me, I'm going to show you how to dance the samba.

Use *look at* to mean observe. There is little or no sense of movement.

Will you look at me when I'm talking to you?
Look at the stars – how beautiful they are tonight.

See is a verb of the senses and refers to one's physical sight. It is generally used with can in this sense.

Can you see my pen anywhere?
I couldn't see you from here.

15.21 False friends

A false friend is a word in one's own language that looks the same as word in another language but has in fact a different meaning. All the false friends listed below are common to at least two European languages; the first, *actually*, is common to nearly all European languages – it only has a different meaning in English!

	MEANS	DOES NOT MEAN
actually	really, in reality	currently, at the moment
agenda	list of things to discuss	diary, note book
argument	heated discussion	subject, topic
assist	help	attend, participate, be present
camping	the act of camping	campsite
canteen	work cafeteria	cellar
comfortable	allowing one to relax	convenient
convenient	suitable, situated nearby	inexpensive
control	exert power, regulate	check, verify
deception	st to make sn believe st else	disappointment
editor	sn who edits texts or is in charge of a newspaper	a publisher
education	what you learn at school	upbringing (what you learn at home)
embarrassed	feel uncomfortable	pregnant
eventually	in the end (after some trouble)	if necessary, in the likely course of events
fabric	cloth, material	factory
genial	friendly	brilliant
history	the events of a country	the events in a work of fiction
journal	a weekly or monthly magazine	a daily newspaper
lecture	a talk giving information	a reading text
library	a place for borrowing books	a place for buying books
local	an adjective meaning near	a pub, night club
lucky	fortunate	happy
magazine	a weekly publication	a store house or warehouse
manifestation	giving a clear example	demonstration
material	fabric, cloth, facts, substance	a subject studied
novel	a book of fiction	a short story
parents	mother and father	relatives

photograph	picture	photographer
physicist	sn who studies physics	doctor, physician
possibly	perhaps, please	if possible
pretend	fake, claim	expect, intend, aspire to
professor	university academic	school teacher
propaganda	false publicity for political aims	advertising
proper	correct, suitable, right	own
public	people in general	audience, spectators
realize	begin to understand	create, develop
regard	be related to	look at
receipt	proof of purchase	recipe (food), prescription (medicine)
sensible	reasonable, practical	sensitive
serious	not humorous	professional
smoking	the act of smoking	a (smoking) jacket
sympathetic	understanding of other's situation	friendly, nice, easy to get on with
technique	method	technology
tonight	the night following today	the night before today
voyage	journey by sea or space	any kind of journey

Sources and Acknowledgements

The first line in each chapter entry refers to the *factoids* or *what the experts say* sections. The numbers in brackets indicate the number of the factoid, e.g. 2) = the second factoid or quotation. If no source is given the information is in the public domain or I have been unable to find the original source. While I have attempted to ensure that the factoids only contain accurate information, I can give no guarantee that the information is 100% accurate.

Any names of people with no further explanations, simply refer to the colleagues and students who provided me with examples of their experience. I am particularly grateful to them.

Chapter 1

My own survey of the web and tweets.

1.4, 1.5 Laura Steven and Anna Southern.

1.6 Lorenzo Ressel and Rômulo Rodrigues

1.9 *Buying a house in Italy*, Gordon Neale, Crimson Publishing, 2008; Tom Southern

1.10 Andrew Flint

1.11 The script comes from an improvised conversation recorded with three actors during recording sessions for the first edition of *International Express Upper Intermediate* (OUP).

1.13 Questions 1-6 were based on questions found in *Dos and Taboos of Hosting International Visitors*, Roger Axtell, Wiley, 1990

© Springer International Publishing Switzerland 2016
A. Wallwork, *English for Interacting on Campus*,
English for Academic Research, DOI 10.1007/978-3-319-28734-8

Acknowledgements: I would like to thank Elena Castanas, Tarun Huria, Sofia Luzgina, Daniel Sentenac, Eriko Tsuchida, and Ting Zheng for providing me with information about their countries.

Chapter 2

All accessed 8 October 2015

1) http://www.hexjam.com/uk/drinking-survey-2015/the-university-drinking-league-2015

2) https://www.teenlife.com/blogs/10-surprising-facts-about-college

3) http://uk.businessinsider.com/colleges-where-youll-meet-your-spouse-2015-5?op=1

4) https://www.quora.com/Why-do-American-students-ask-more-questions-in-class-than-Asian-students

5) http://www.societies.cam.ac.uk/

6) https://en.wikipedia.org/wiki/List_of_largest_universities_by_enrollment

7) http://www.economist.com/blogs/dailychart/2011/09/female-graduation-rates

8) http://en.russia.edu.ru/faq/2579/

9) https://en.wikipedia.org/wiki/Higher_education_in_Japan#University_entrance

10) http://www.dailymail.co.uk/news/article-2404988/Child-prodigy-Carson-Huey-You-11-starts-semester-college-studying-quantum-physics.html

2.4 Transcript of a recording of a conversation with Mary Harding.

Chapter 3

All from *1001 Things Every College Student Needs to Know* written by Harry Harrison Jr and reproduced with the kind permission of Thomas Nelson.

3.4 Claudia Scattino, Zahra Moharrer, Margherita Mencattelli

3.12 Misty Cozac

3.14 http://magazine.thenews.com.pk/mag/detail_article.asp?magId=1&id=8719 (this link also contains the answer to the student's letter

Chapter 4

spikedmath.com/092.html - please could the copyright holders contact me.

Chapter 5

1 and **2:** Business Options, Adrian Wallwork, OUP; **3-7**: http://www.brainyquote. com

5.1 1-6): *Academic Interactions,* Feak, Reinhart, Rohlck, Michigan Series in English for Academic & Professional Purposes **8)** *The impact of culture on student attributions for performance: A comparative study of three groups of EFL/ESL learners,* Peter Gobel, JIRSEA Vol 9 No 1 May/June 2011; survey of business executives reported in *Business Options*, Adrian Wallwork, OUP

5.10 *Business Options*, Adrian Wallwork, OUP

Chapter 6

http://www.economist.com/blogs/johnson/2011/05/euphemistically_speaking

6.1 The Book of Chance, John Hodgson, Weidenfeld & Nicolson, 199; Dr Sue Fraser with kind permission from the author

6.2 *Attention breaks in lectures*, Johnstone and Percival, Education in Chemistry, 13: 49-50

6.11 The statistics are reported in *Presenting with Power*, Shay McConnon, How to Books, 2002; and in *Persuasion: The Art of Influencing People*, James Borg, Pearson 2004, respectively.

Chapter 7

1-3) *The Penguin International Thesaurus of Quotations*, ed. Rhoda Toma Tripp, Penguin Books., **4)** *The Penguin Dictionary of Modern Quotations*, ed. J M and M J Cohen, Penguin Books; **5-6)** *Handbook of 20th Century Quotations*, ed Frank S Pepper, Sphere Books Ltd; **7)** *The Arab Executive*, Farid Muna, Palgrave Macmillan, 1980.

Chapter 8

The telephone dates from 1876 to 2000 come from the following sources Wikipedia, Daily Express (12 March 2001, article by William Harston); *The First of Everything*, Dennis Sanders, Delacorte Press; *Architects of the Business Revolution*, Des Dearlove and Stephen Coomber, Capstone; from 2003-2014 from the web, and the

last two dates from my imagination. There appears to be some contrasting information with regard to when the first phone call was made and the first phones were
sold.

8.1 Patrick Forsyth, Touchstone Training & Consultancy; Susan B. Barnes,
Associate Director, Lab for Social Computing, Rochester Institute of Technology

Chapter 9

1) data derived from World Tourism Organization **2)** British Council, http://www.
msnbc.msn.com/id/7038031/site/newsweek/, **4)** http://www.gallup.com/poll/1825/
about-one-four-americans-can-hold-conversation-second-language.aspx;   http://
www.guardian.co.uk/education/2010/aug/24/who-still-wants-learn-languages;
http://www.britac.ac.uk/policy/language-matters/position-paper.cfm; **5)** Talkworks
at work (British Telecom), by Gerard Egan and Andrew Bailey, available for free
download   at: http://www.numberoneskill.com/number1skill/archive/media.
ikml?PHPSESSID= 0c6c664d7781ffae89e6c75332183b95; **6)** The study is reported
in D. Bone, *A Practical Guide to Effective Listening*, Kogan Page.

9.1 *World's greatest book of useless information*, Noel Botham, Perigee Books,
2009; *Why men don't listen and Women Can't Read Maps*, Allan Pease and Barbara
Pease, Harmony 2001; Daily Mail]

Chapter 10

1) Data taken from Sue Fraser's article "Perceptions of varieties of spoken English:
implications for EIL" and reproduced by kind permission of the author. **3)** Korea:
Read the full article at: http://www.independent.co.uk/news/world/asia/seoul-tries-
to-shock-parents-out-of-linguistic-surgery-573153.html

Chapter 12

2) most comes from this site: http://ec.europa.eu/education/languages/index_en.htm.

Chapter 14

1-2) *The English Language, Essays by English & American Men of Letters 1490–
1839*, ed. W.F. Bolton, 1966, Cambridge University Press; **3-4)** *Handbook of 20th
Century Quotations*, ed Frank S Pepper, Sphere Books Ltd.

14.1 *Academic Interactions,* Feak, Reinhart, Rohlck, Michigan Series in English for
Academic & Professional Purposes

Index

Numbers in **bold** refer to complete chapters (e.g. **5** = Chapter 5), numbers not in bold refer to subsections (e.g. 5.7 = Section 7 in Chapter 5).